GALWAY
STREET ATLAS

Gaillimh
Atlas Sráide

CONTENTS

MAP PAGES	1 - 48
CITY CENTRE MAP	49 - 50
TOURIST INFORMATION	51 - 57
INDEX	58 - 61

COMPILED, PRINTED AND PUBLISHED BY
ORDNANCE SURVEY IRELAND, PHOENIX PARK, DUBLIN 8.

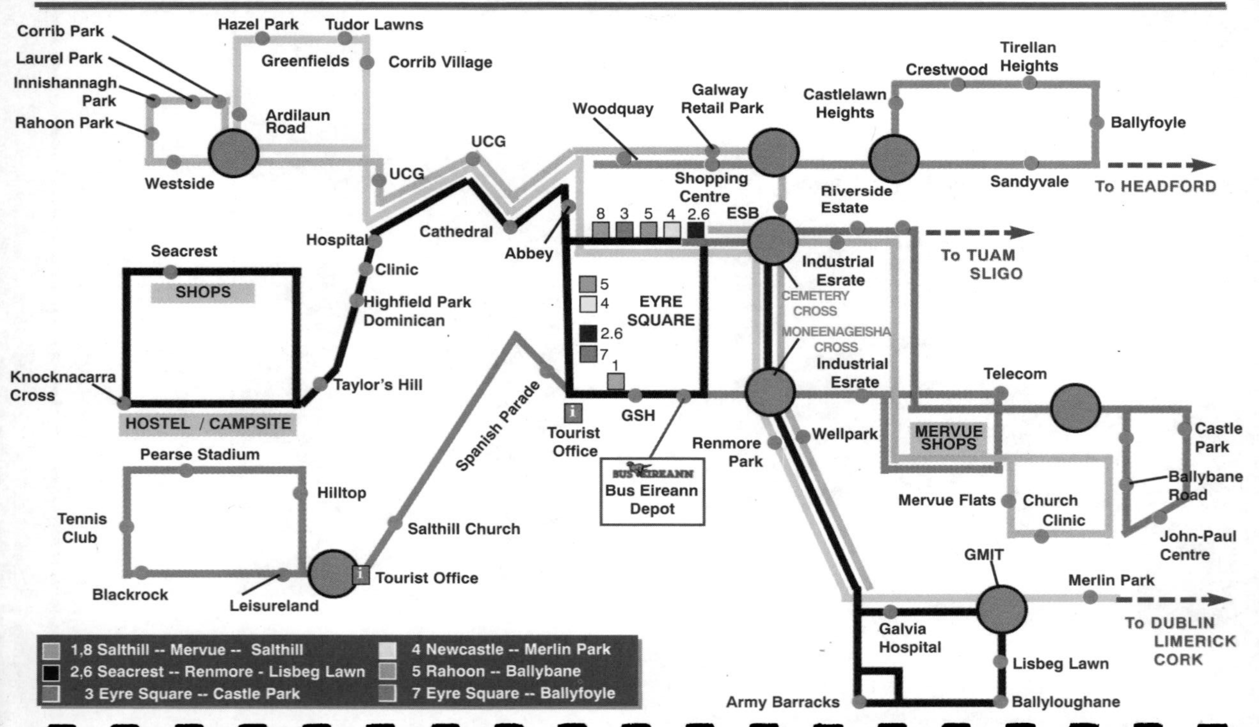
BUS EIREANN
GALWAY CITY BUS SERVICES
Corrib Park
Laurel Park
Innishannagh Park
Rahoon Park
Westside
Ardilaun Road
Hazel Park
Tudor Lawns
Greenfields
Corrib Village
UCG
UCG
Hospital
Clinic
Highfield Park
Dominican
Taylor's Hill
Cathedral
Abbey
Seacrest
SHOPS
Knocknacarra Cross
HOSTEL / CAMPSITE
Pearse Stadium
Hilltop
Tennis Club
Blackrock
Leisureland
Tourist Office
Salthill Church
Spanish Parade
Tourist Office
GSH
Bus Eireann Depot
Woodquay
Galway Retail Park
Shopping Centre
ESB
8 3 5 4 2.6
EYRE SQUARE
5
4
2.6
7
1
Castlelawn Heights
Crestwood
Tirellan Heights
Ballyfoyle
Sandyvale
To HEADFORD
Riverside Estate
To TUAM SLIGO
Industrial Esrate
CEMETERY CROSS
MONEENAGEISHA CROSS
Industrial Esrate
Renmore Park
Wellpark
Telecom
MERVUE SHOPS
Mervue Flats
Church
Clinic
Castle Park
Ballybane Road
John-Paul Centre
GMIT
Merlin Park
To DUBLIN LIMERICK CORK
Galvia Hospital
Lisbeg Lawn
Army Barracks
Ballyloughane
1,8 Salthill -- Mervue -- Salthill
2,6 Seacrest -- Renmore - Lisbeg Lawn
3 Eyre Square -- Castle Park
4 Newcastle -- Merlin Park
5 Rahoon -- Ballybane
7 Eyre Square -- Ballyfoyle

LEGEND

- MAIN ROADS/ STREETS
- OTHER ROADS/ STREETS (UNNAMED)
- NARROW / STREET PRIVATE ROADS
- PEDESTRIAN STREETS
- BUILT UP AREA
- PUBLIC PARK
- PUBLIC BUILDING
- RAIL/ BUS STATION
- BUILDING OF NOTE
- HOSPITAL
- WATER

- CINEMA
- SHOPPING COMPLEX
- ART GALLERY
- MUSEUM
- VISITOR CENTRE
- LIBRARY
- CHURCH OF NOTE
- BUILDING OF SPECIAL INTEREST
- 3RD LEVEL INST.
- GAELIC GROUND
- RUGBY GROUND
- SOCCER GROUND

- THEATRE
- TOURIST OFFICE
- EMERGENCY HOSPITAL
- INDEPENDENT HOSTEL
- AN ÓIGE HOSTEL
- POST OFFICE
- PARKING
- GARDA
- FIRE STATION
- MAINLINE RAIL STATION
- ONE WAY TRAFFIC SYSTEM
- CHURCH

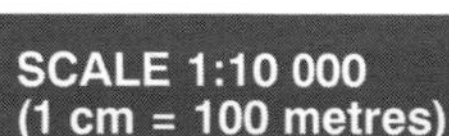
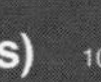
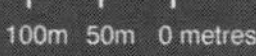

SCALE 1:10 000
(1 cm = 100 metres)

100m 50m 0 metres 100m 200m 300m 400m 500 metres

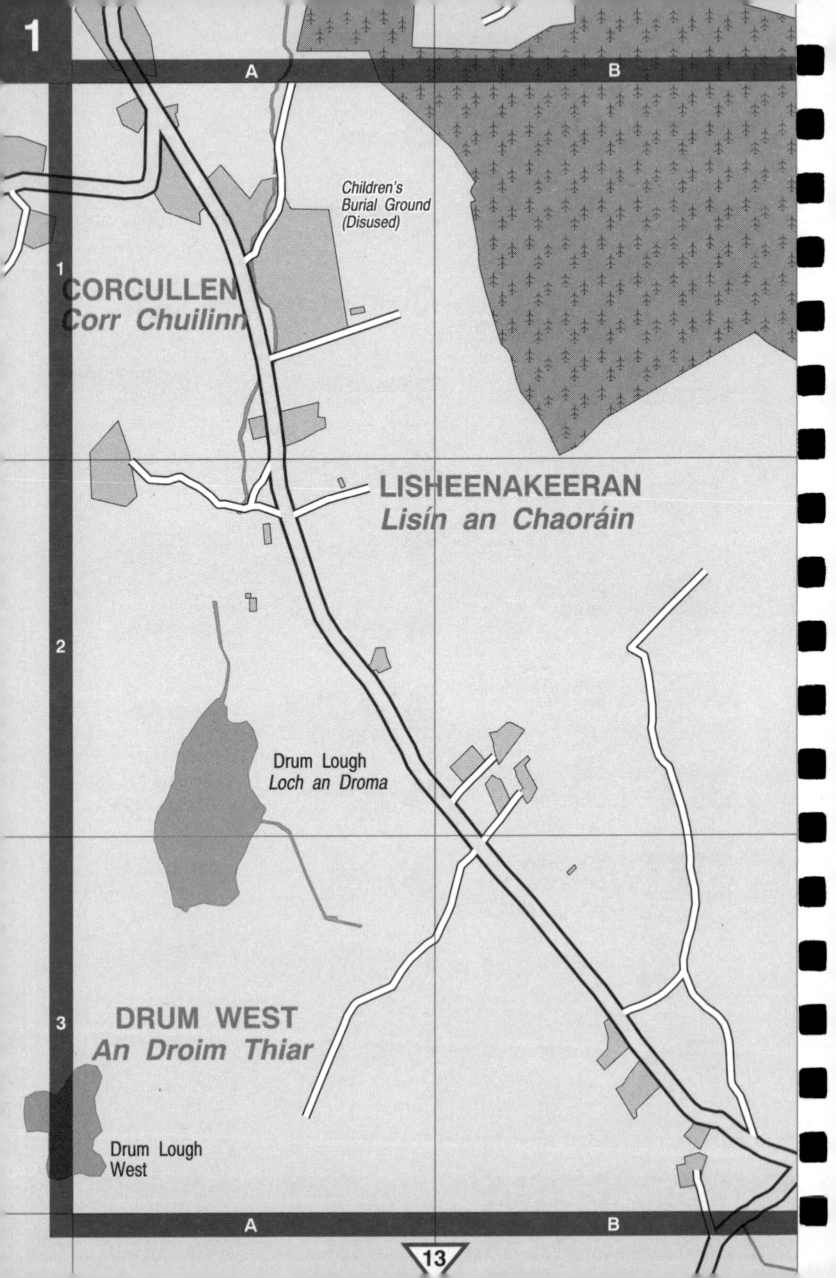
1
A
B
Children's
Burial Ground
(Disused)
1
CORCULLEN
Corr Chuilinn
LISHEENAKEERAN
Lisín an Chaoráin
2
Drum Lough
Loch an Droma
3
DRUM WEST
An Droim Thiar
Drum Lough
West
A
B

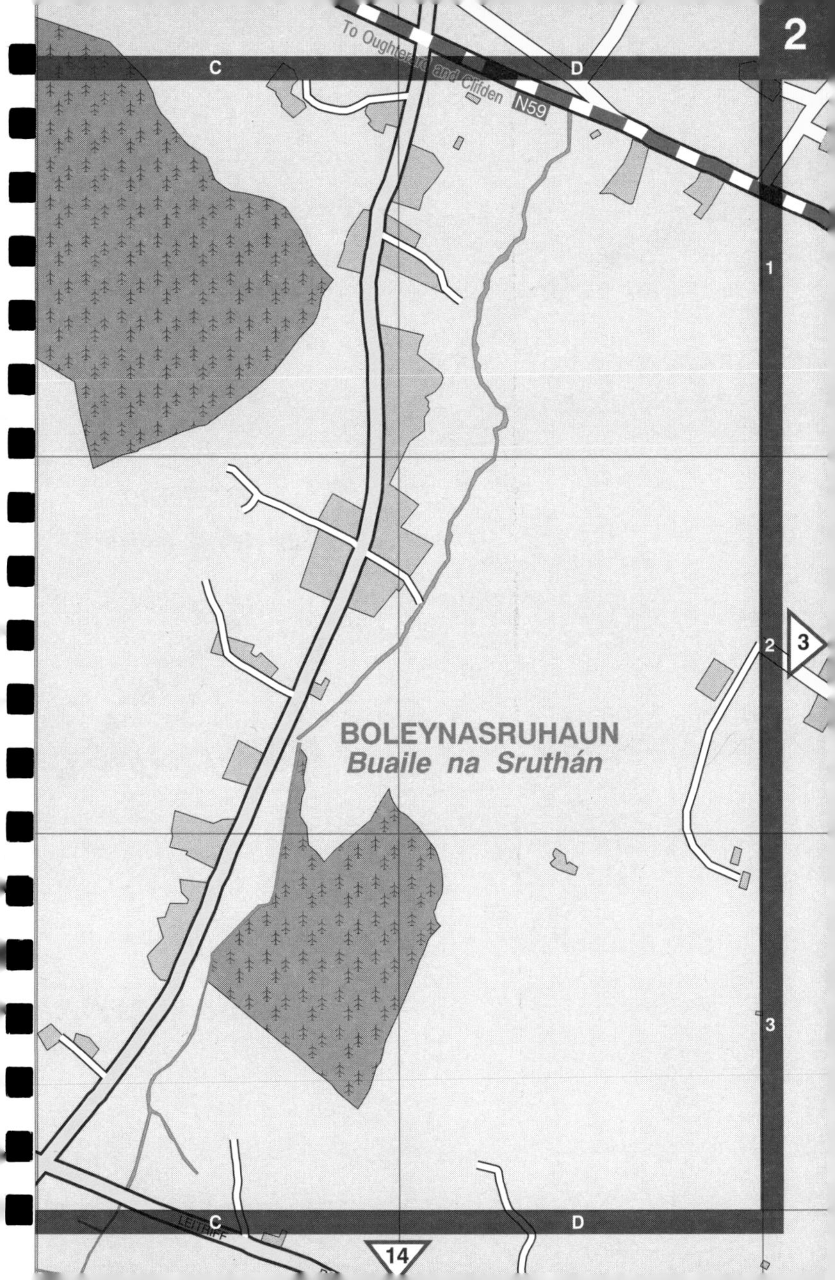

To Oughterard and Clifden
N59
C
D
1
2
3
3
BOLEYNASRUHAUN
Buaile na Sruthán
LEITRIFF
C
D
14

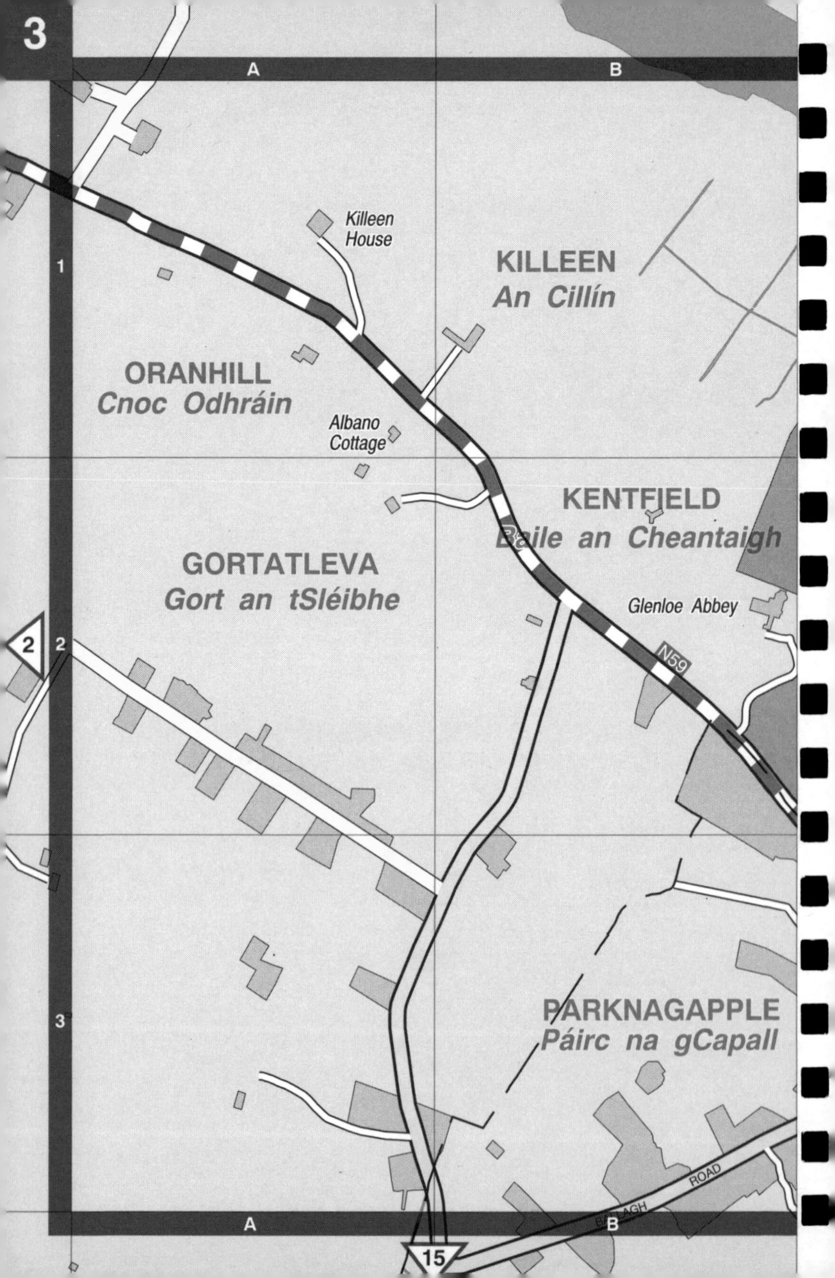
A
B
1
2
3
Killeen
House
KILLEEN
An Cillín
ORANHILL
Cnoc Odhráin
Albano
Cottage
KENTFIELD
Baile an Cheantaigh
GORTATLEVA
Gort an tSléibhe
Glenloe Abbey
N59
PARKNAGAPPLE
Páirc na gCapall
BALLAGH ROAD
A
B
2
15

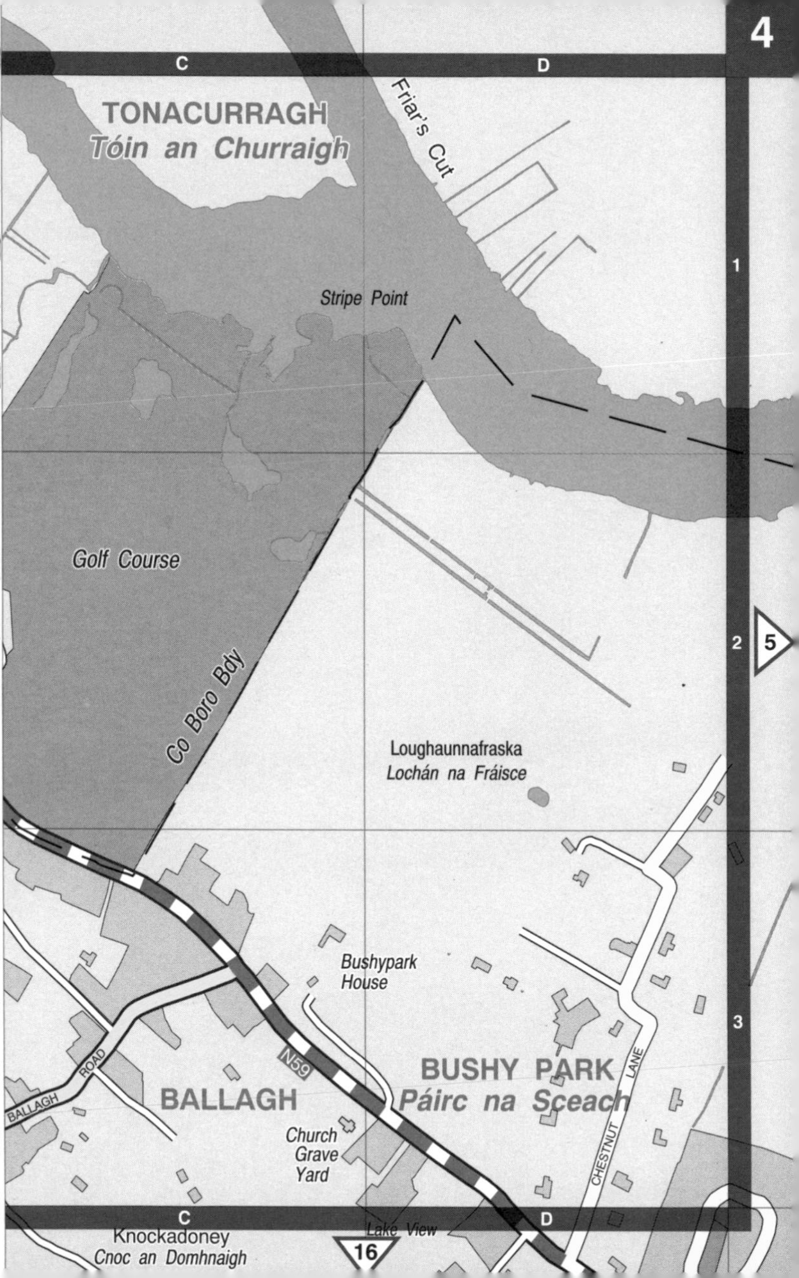

C D

TONACURRAGH
Tóin an Churraigh

Friar's Cut

Stripe Point

1

Golf Course

Co Boro Bdy

2 5

Loughaunnafraska
Lochán na Fráisce

Bushypark
House

3

N59

BUSHY PARK
Páirc na Sceach

BALLAGH

BALLAGH ROAD

CHESTNUT LANE

Church
Grave
Yard

C D

Knockadoney
Cnoc an Domhnaigh

Lake View

16

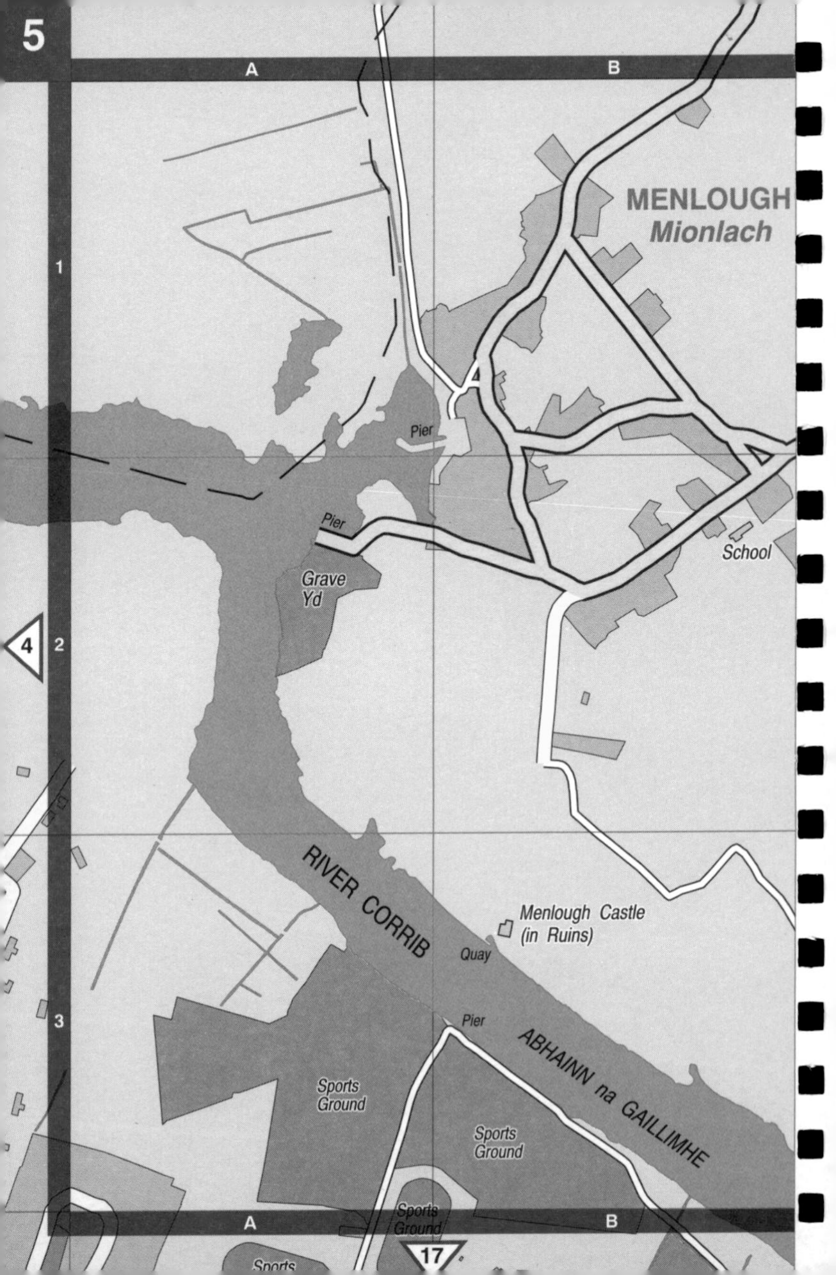
5
A
B
MENLOUGH
Mionlach
1
Pier
Pier
Grave
Yd
School
2
4
RIVER CORRIB
Menlough Castle
(in Ruins)
Quay
Pier
3
ABHAINN na GAILLIMHE
Sports
Ground
Sports
Ground
Sports
Ground
A
B
17

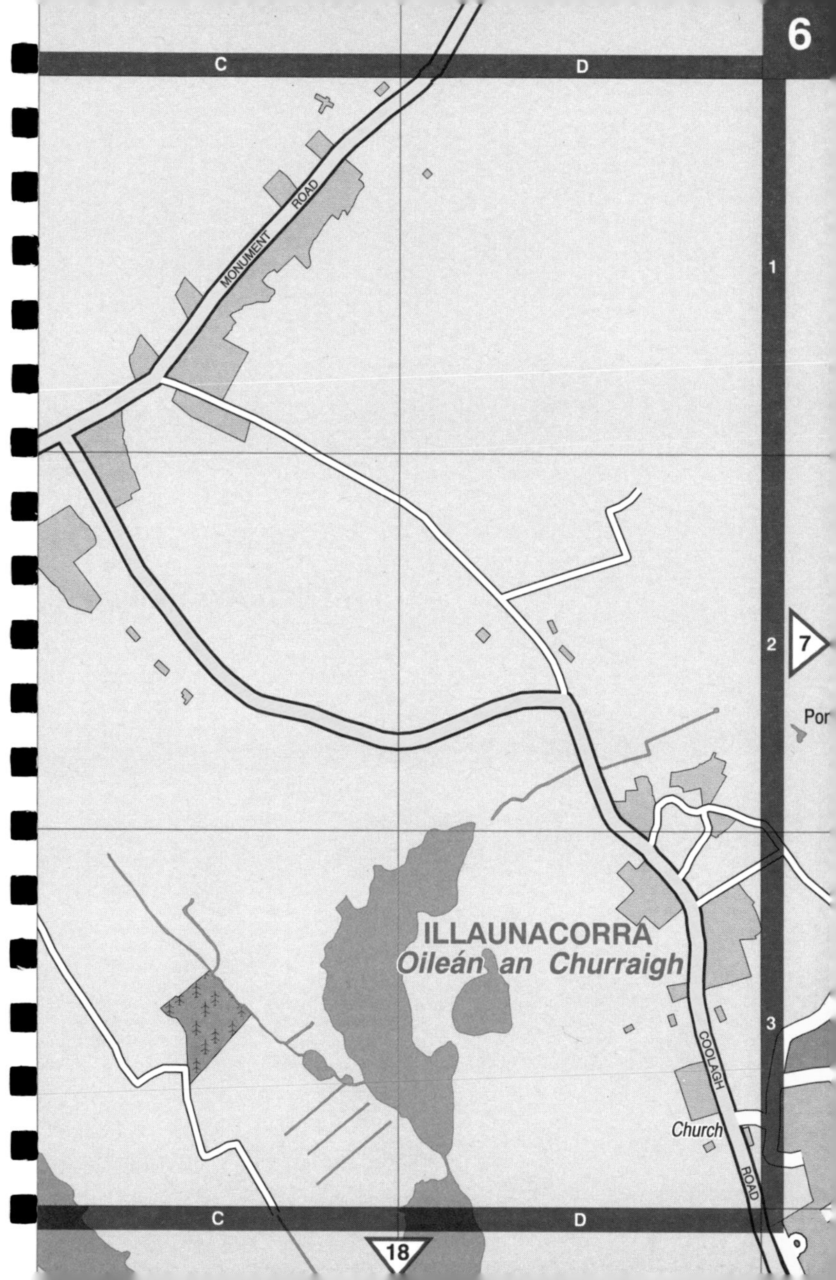
6
C
D
MONUMENT
ROAD
1
2
7
Por
ILLAUNACORRA
Oileán an Churraigh
3
COOLAGH
ROAD
Church
C
D
18

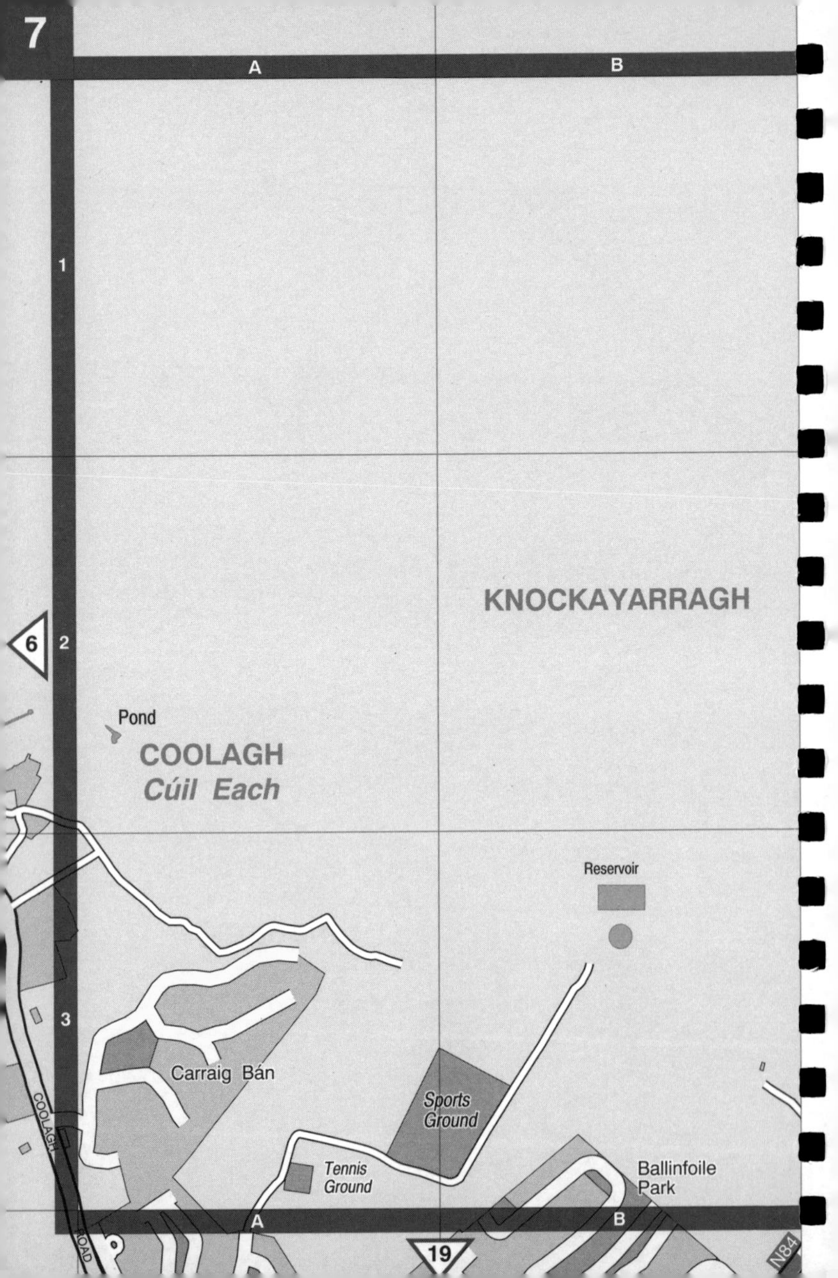
A
B
1
2
3
6
KNOCKAYARRAGH
Pond
COOLAGH
Cúil Each
Reservoir
Carraig Bán
Sports Ground
Tennis Ground
Ballinfoile Park
COOLAGH ROAD
A
B
19
N84

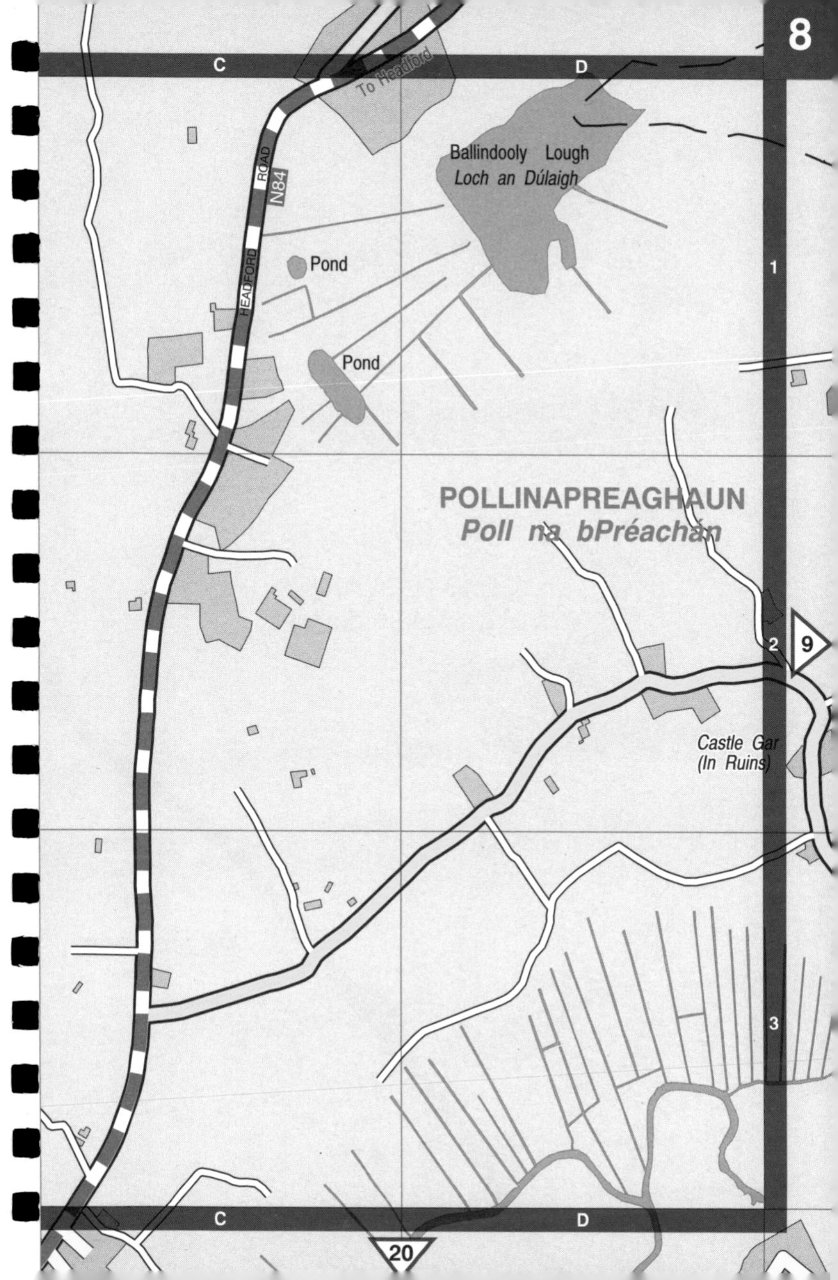

8
C
D
To Headford
Ballindooly Lough
Loch an Dúlaigh
HEADFORD ROAD
N84
Pond
Pond
1
POLLINAPREAGHAUN
Poll na bPréachán
2
9
Castle Gar
(In Ruins)
3
C
D
20

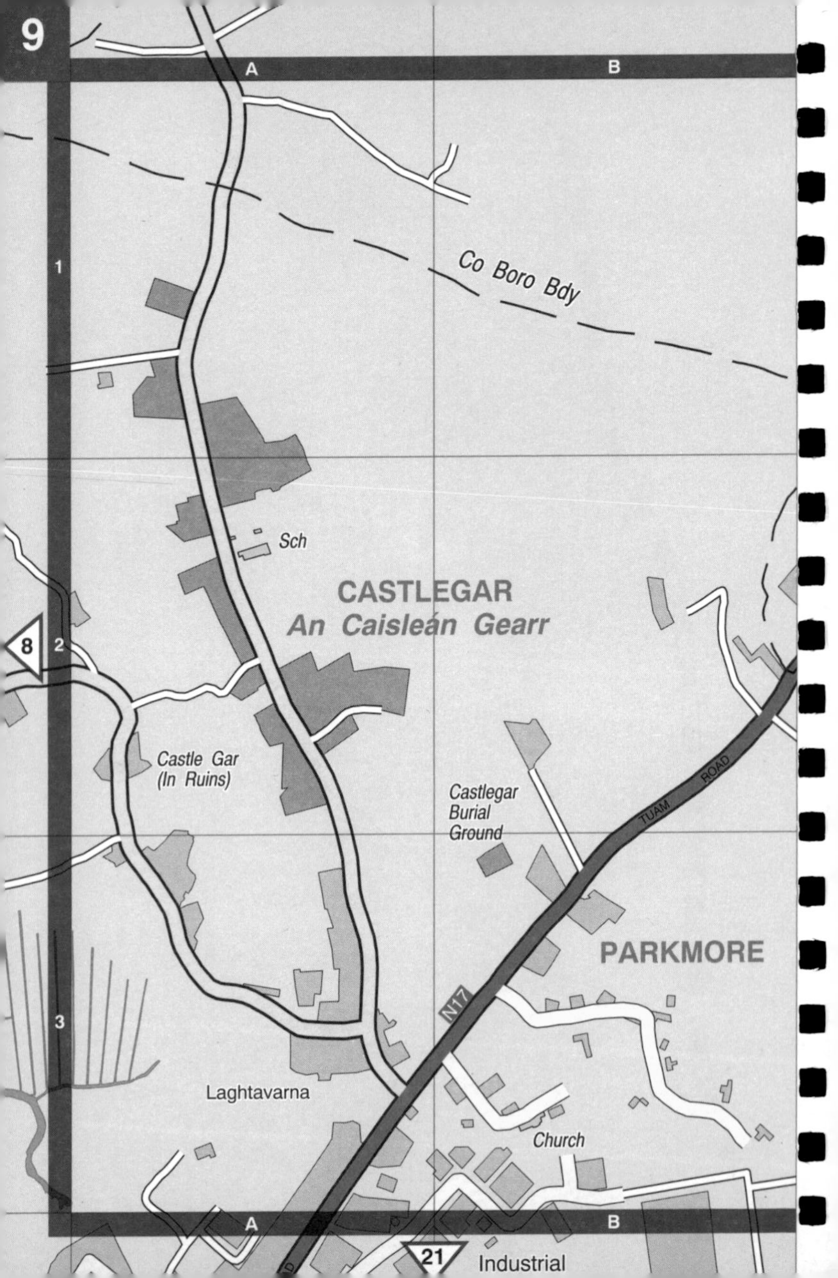
A
B
1
2
3
8
Co Boro Bdy
Sch
CASTLEGAR
An Caisleán Gearr
Castle Gar
(In Ruins)
Castlegar
Burial
Ground
TUAM ROAD
N17
PARKMORE
Laghtavarna
Church
A
B
21
Industrial

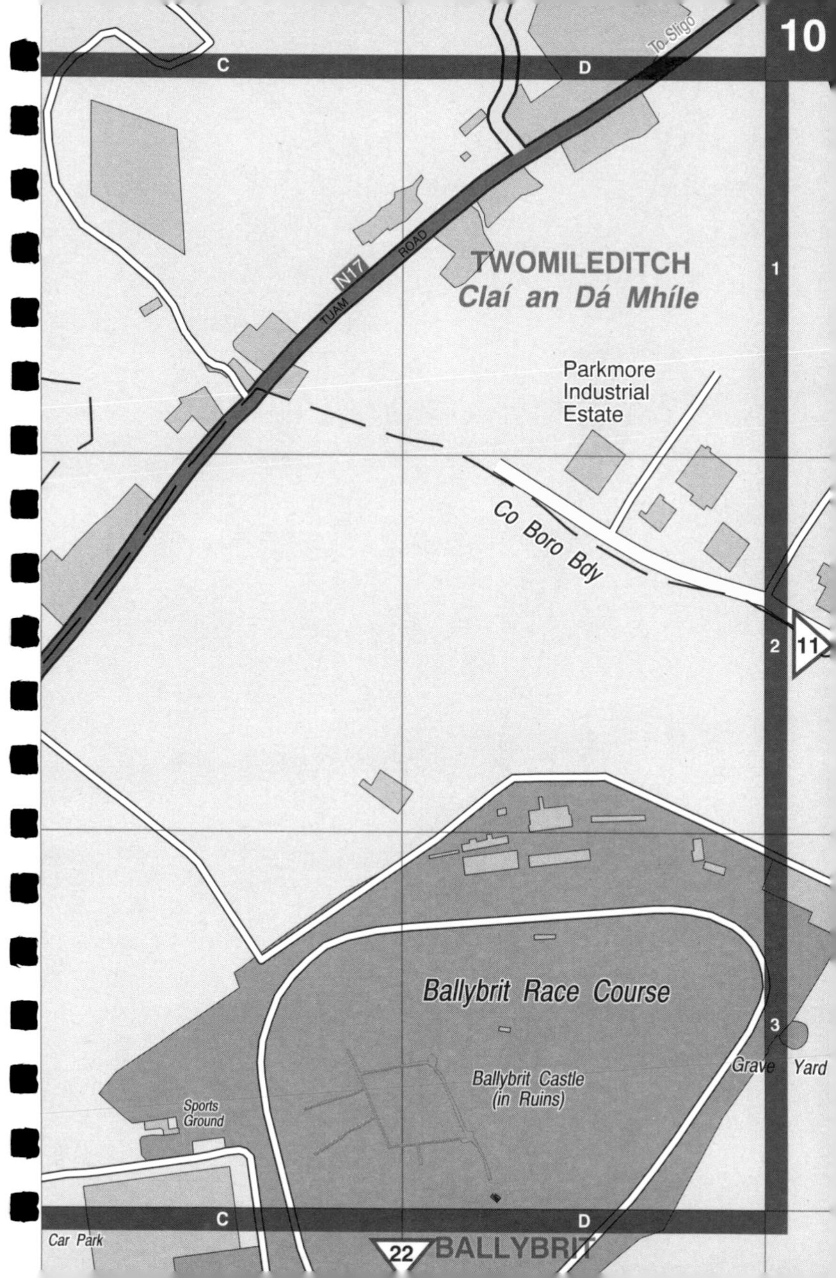
C
D
To Sligo
N17
TUAM ROAD
TWOMILEDITCH
Claí an Dá Mhíle
1
Parkmore
Industrial
Estate
Co Boro Bdy
2
11
Ballybrit Race Course
3
Grave Yard
Ballybrit Castle
(in Ruins)
Sports
Ground
C
D
Car Park
22
BALLYBRIT

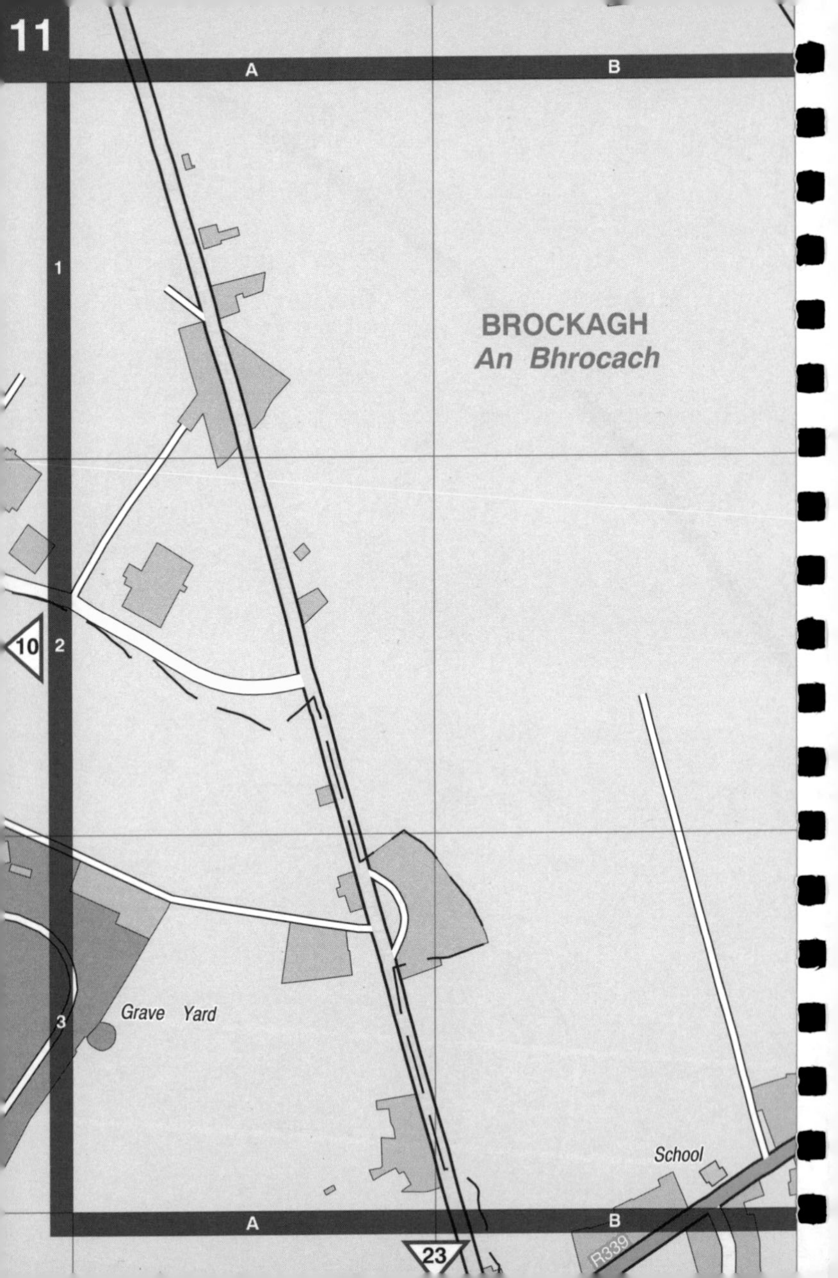
A
B
1
BROCKAGH
An Bhrocach
10
2
Grave Yard
3
School
A
B
R339
23

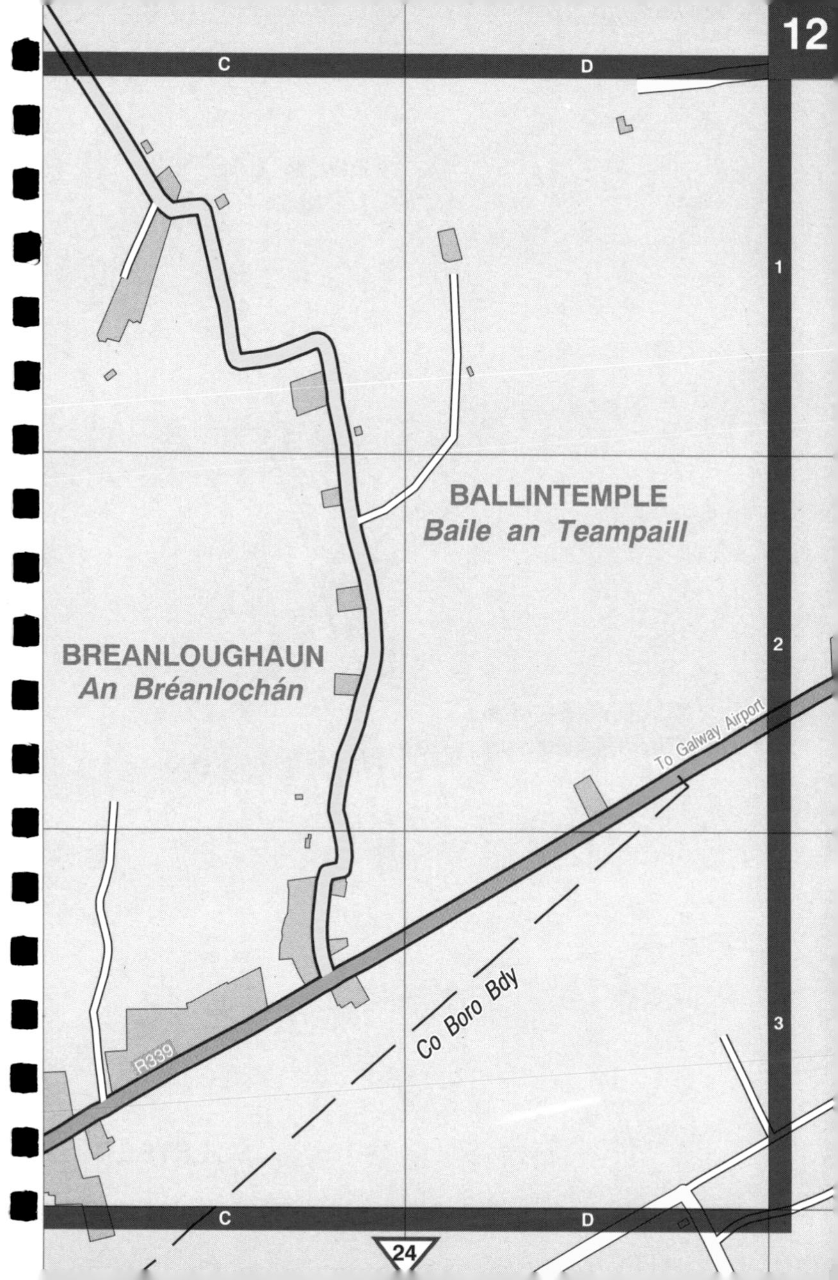
C
D
1
2
3
BALLINTEMPLE
Baile an Teampaill
BREANLOUGHAUN
An Bréanlochán
To Galway Airport
R339
Co Boro Bdy
C
D

24

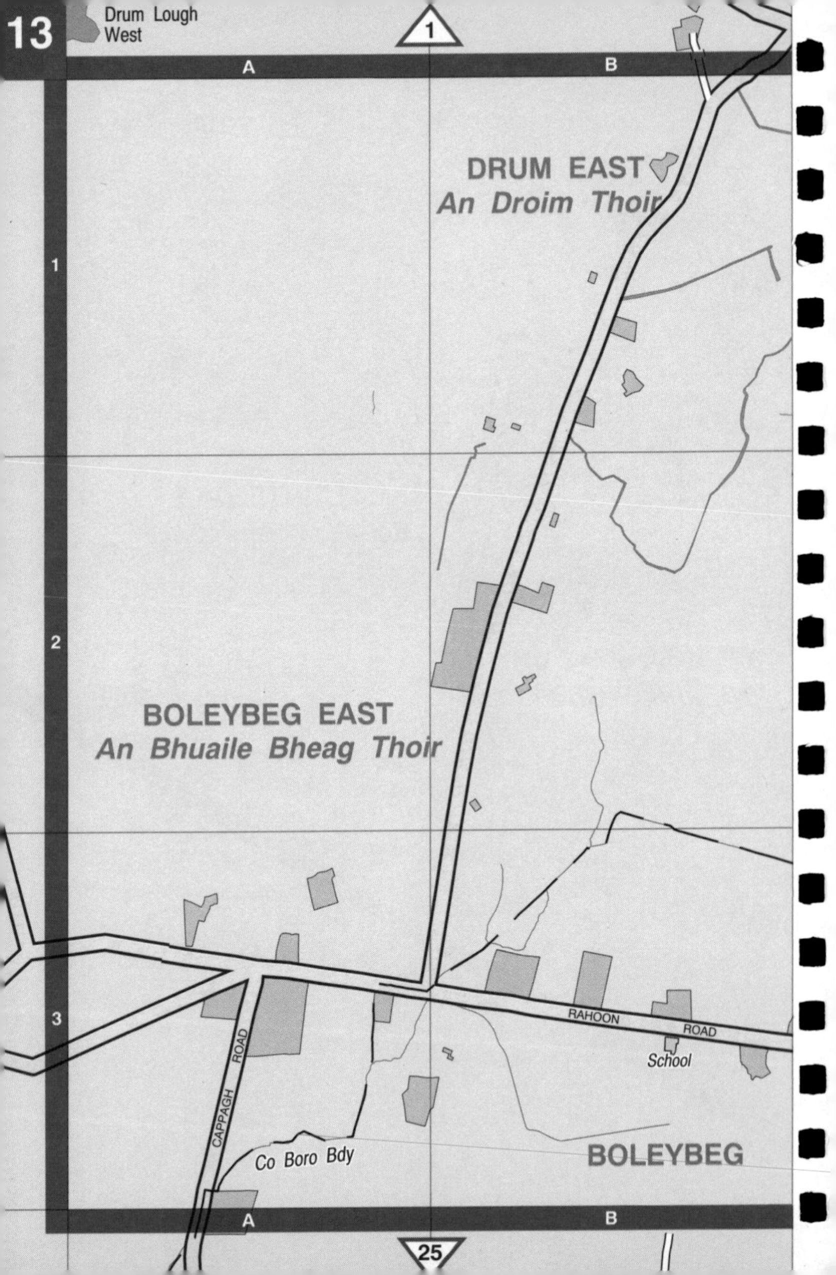
13
Drum Lough West
1
A
B
DRUM EAST
An Droim Thoir
1
2
BOLEYBEG EAST
An Bhuaile Bheag Thoir
3
RAHOON ROAD
School
CAPPAGH ROAD
Co Boro Bdy
BOLEYBEG
A
B
25

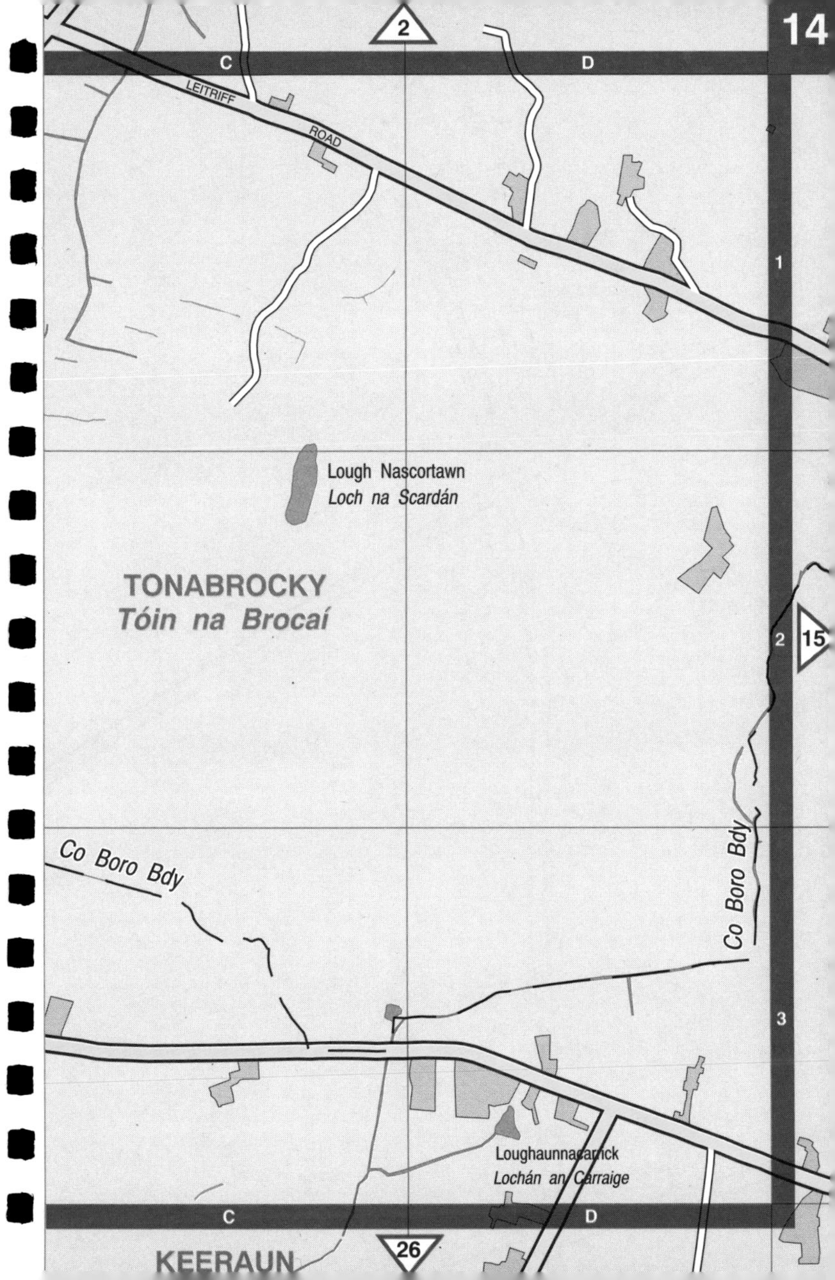
2
C
D
LEITRIFF
ROAD
1
Lough Nascortawn
Loch na Scardán
TONABROCKY
Tóin na Brocaí
2
15
Co Boro Bdy
Co Boro Bdy
3
Loughaunnacarrick
Lochán an Carraige
C
D
26
KEERAUN

3
A
B
BALLAGH
1
Lough Nabrocky
Loch na Brocaí
Lough Beg
An Loch Beag
14
2
Co Boro Bdy
3
A
B
27

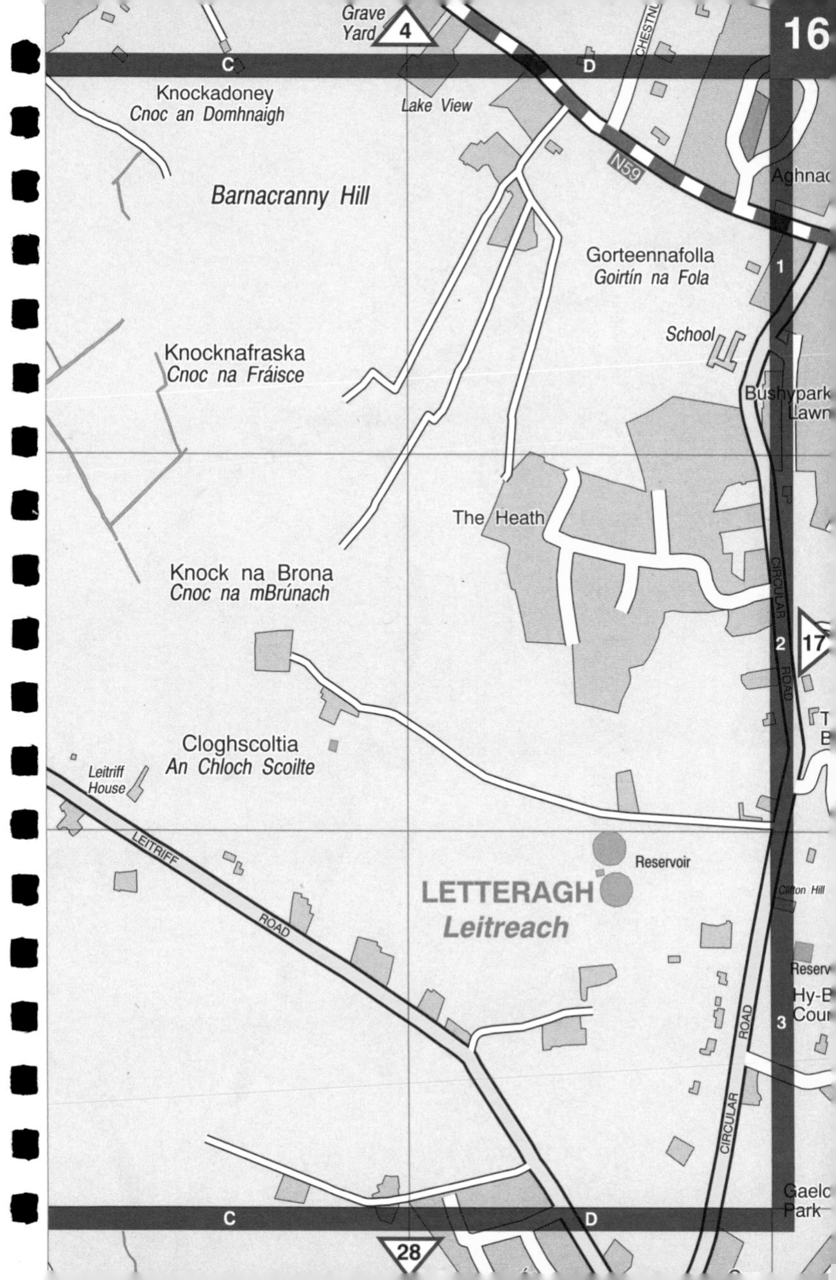
Grave Yard
4
C
D
Knockadoney
Cnoc an Domhnaigh
Lake View
N59
Barnacranny Hill
Gorteennafolla
Goirtín na Fola
1
School
Knocknafraska
Cnoc na Fráisce
The Heath
CIRCULAR ROAD
2
17
Knock na Brona
Cnoc na mBrúnach
Cloghscoltia
An Chloch Scoilte
Leitriff House
LEITRIFF ROAD
Reservoir
LETTERAGH
Leitreach
Clifton Hill
3
CIRCULAR ROAD
C
D
28

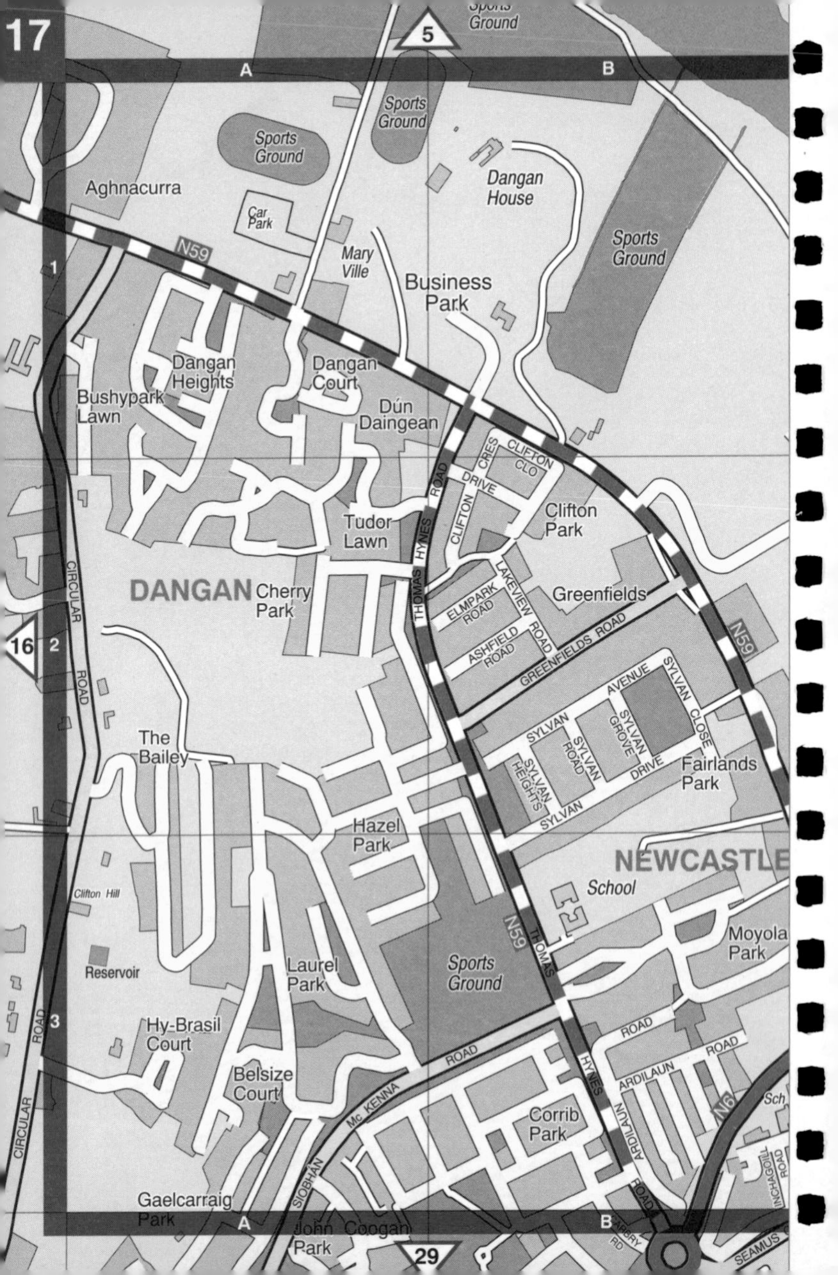
5
A
B
Sports Ground
Sports Ground
Sports Ground
Aghnacurra
Car Park
N59
Mary Ville
Business Park
Dangan House
Sports Ground
Dangan Heights
Dangan Court
Bushypark Lawn
Dún Daingean
CLIFTON CRES
CLIFTON CLO
CLIFTON DRIVE
CLIFTON
Clifton Park
THOMAS HYNES ROAD
Tudor Lawn
DANGAN
Cherry Park
ELMPARK ROAD
LAKEVIEW ROAD
Greenfields
ASHFIELD ROAD
GREENFIELDS ROAD
CIRCULAR ROAD
16
2
1
N59
SYLVAN AVENUE
SYLVAN CLOSE
SYLVAN ROAD
SYLVAN GROVE
SYLVAN DRIVE
SYLVAN HEIGHTS
SYLVAN
Fairlands Park
The Bailey
Hazel Park
NEWCASTLE
School
Clifton Hill
N59
THOMAS
Sports Ground
Moyola Park
Reservoir
Laurel Park
3
ROAD
Hy-Brasil Court
ROAD
ROAD
ROAD
ARDILAUN
Mc KENNA
Belsize Court
HYNES
ARDILAUN
N6
Sch
CIRCULAR
Corrib Park
INCHAGOILL ROAD
SIOBHÁN
Gaelcarraig Park
ROAD
A
B
John Coogan Park
CARBRY RD
SEAMUS
29

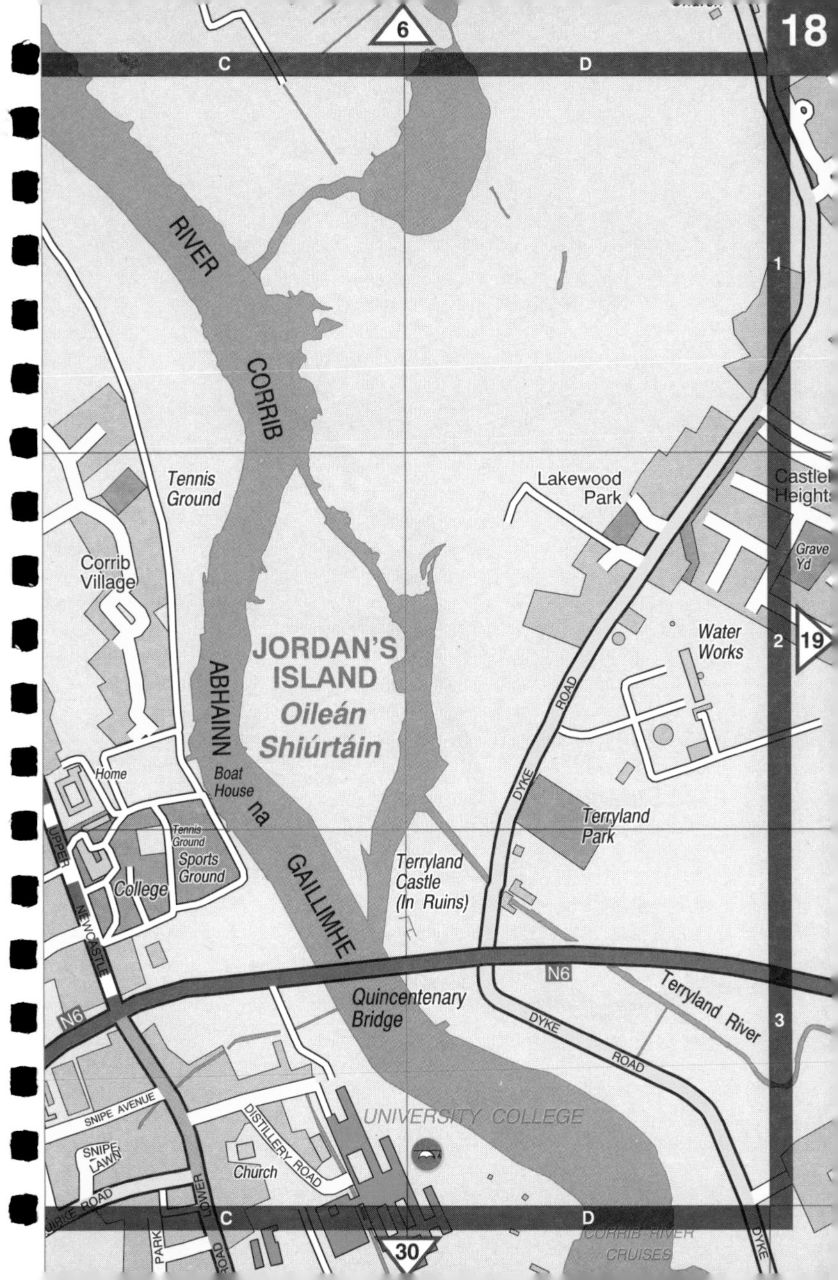
6
C
D
RIVER
CORRIB
Tennis
Ground
Corrib
Village
JORDAN'S
ISLAND
Oileán
Shiúrtáin
ABHAINN
na
GAILLIMHE
Boat
House
Home
Tennis
Ground
Sports
Ground
College
UPPER
NEWCASTLE
Terryland
Castle
(In Ruins)
Lakewood
Park
Castle
Heights
Grave
Yd
Water
Works
19
DYKE
ROAD
Terryland
Park
N6
Quincentenary
Bridge
Terryland River
DYKE
ROAD
SNIPE AVENUE
SNIPE
LAWN
DISTILLERY ROAD
Church
UNIVERSITY COLLEGE
LOWER
ROAD
PARK
CORRIB RIVER
CRUISES
DYKE
30
1
2
3

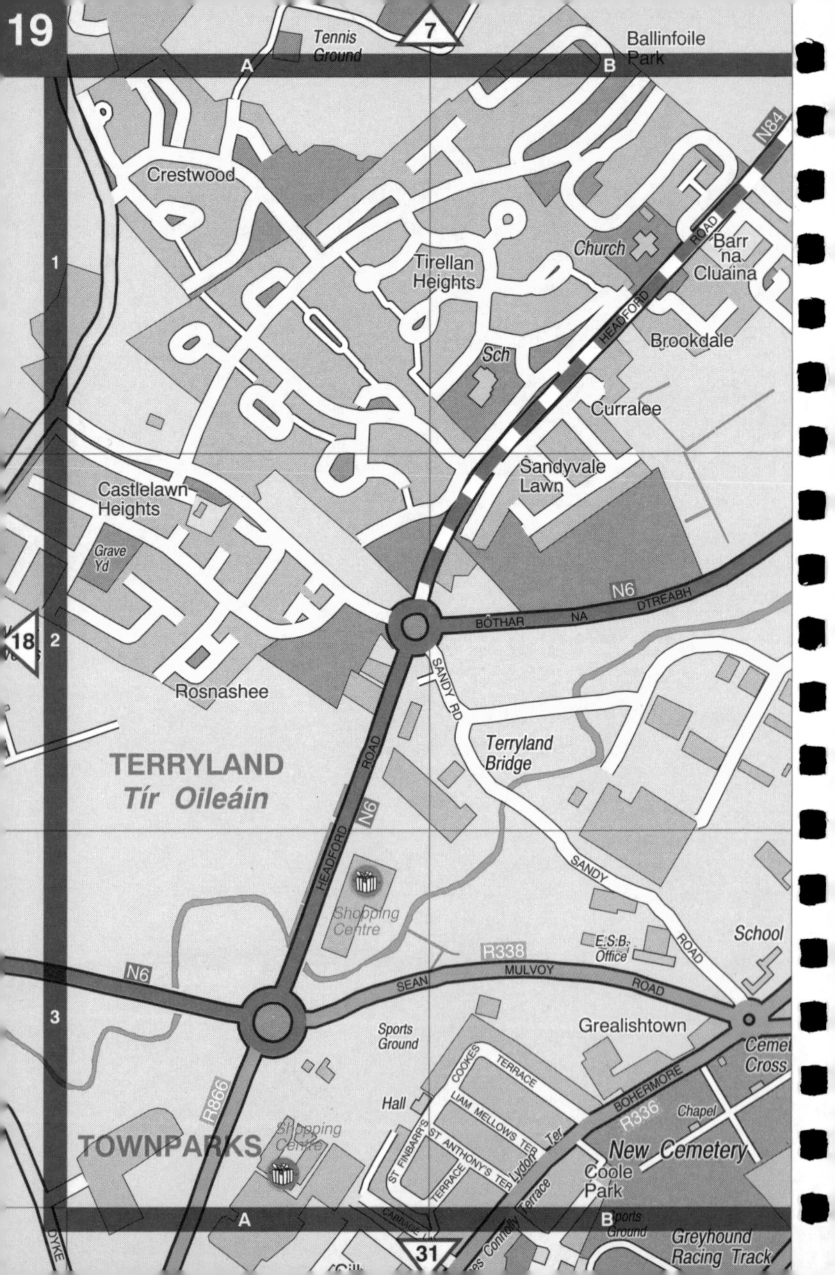
7
Tennis Ground
Ballinfoile Park
A
B
N84
Crestwood
Church
Barr na Cluaina
Tirellan Heights
HEADFORD ROAD
Brookdale
Sch
Curralee
Sandyvale Lawn
Castlelawn Heights
Grave Yd
N6
BÓTHAR NA DTREABH
18
1
2
Rosnashee
SANDY RD
Terryland Bridge
TERRYLAND
Tír Oileáin
HEADFORD ROAD
N6
SANDY ROAD
Shopping Centre
School
E.S.B. Office
R338
N6
SEAN MULVOY ROAD
3
Sports Ground
Grealishtown
Cemet Cross
COOKES TERRACE
R866
Hall
LIAM MELLOWS TER
BOHERMORE
R336
Chapel
Shopping Centre
TOWNPARKS
ST ANTHONY'S TER
ST FINBARR'S TERRACE
Lydon Ter
New Cemetery
Coole Park
Terrace
CABBAGE
Connolly Terrace
Sports Ground
Greyhound Racing Track
DYKE
31

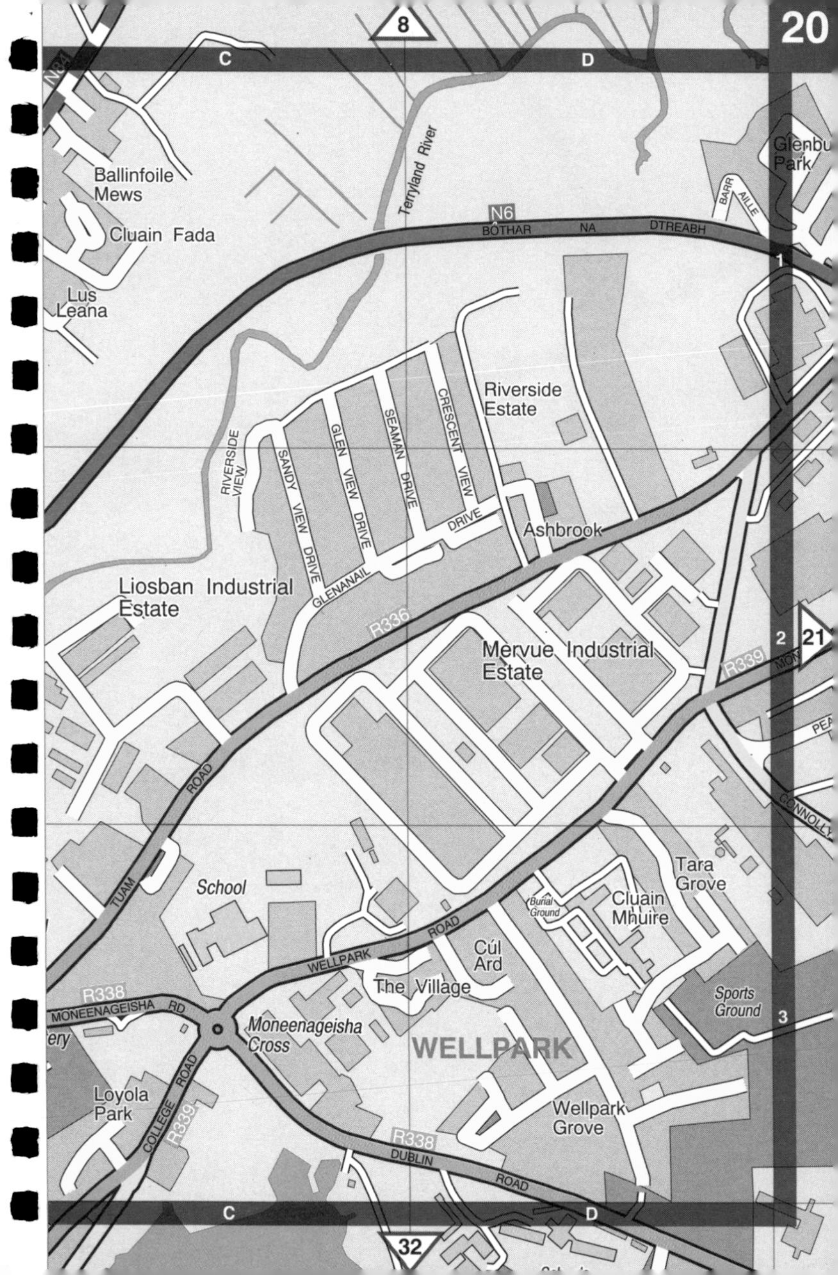

8
C
D
N84
Ballinfoile Mews
Cluain Fada
Lus Leana
Terryland River
Glenbu Park
BARR AILLE
N6
BÓTHAR NA DTREABH
1
Riverside Estate
RIVERSIDE VIEW
SANDY VIEW DRIVE
GLEN VIEW DRIVE
SEAMAN DRIVE
CRESCENT VIEW
DRIVE
Ashbrook
GLENANAIL
Liosban Industrial Estate
R336
Mervue Industrial Estate
2
21
R339
MON
PEA
ROAD
CONNOLLY
TUAM
School
Tara Grove
Burial Ground
Cluain Mhuire
ROAD
Cúl Ard
WELLPARK
The Village
R338
MONEENAGEISHA RD
Moneenageisha Cross
Sports Ground
3
WELLPARK
Loyola Park
COLLEGE ROAD
R339
Wellpark Grove
R338
DUBLIN ROAD
C
D
32

9
A
B
Industrial
Estate
Glenburren
Park
N17
TUAM
ROAD
BARR AILLE
1
N6
BÓTHAR NA DTREABH
R336
N6
R339
MONIVEA
BALLYBAAN
Telephone
Exchange
Monivea
Park
ROAD
R339
MONIVEA
20
2
McDONAGH
CLARK
AVENUE
AVENUE
KENT AVE
EMMET AVENUE
AVENUE
PEARSE AVENUE
PARNELL AVENUE
TONE AVE
PLUNKETT
PO
McDERMOTT AVENUE
BARRY AVENUE
McBRIDE AVENUE
MALLIN AVE
McHUGH AVENUE
CONNOLLY AVENUE
BALLYBAAN ROAD
R865
BALLYBAAN ROAD
Sports
Ground
ROCKLANDS AVE
ROCKLAND'S AVE
Souterrain
Shopping
Centre
MEADOW GROVE
Beechwood
Park
ARD AOIBHINN DRIVE
HEATHER GRO
Rahylin
Glebe
MICHAEL COLLINS ROAD
Mervue Sports
Centre
Sports
Ground
3
Walter Macken
Place
WALTER MACKEN ROAD
Hostel
ARD AOIBHINN DR
Church
School
Bay
View
Rise
QUINN TERRACE
QUINN PL
LOUGHNANE TER
LOUGHNANE PL
ST JAMES ROAD
Health
Centre
St James
Crescent
Bay
View
Heights
Rahylin
Glebe
A
B
CARDINAL CUSHING RD
R338
Grave
Yd
33

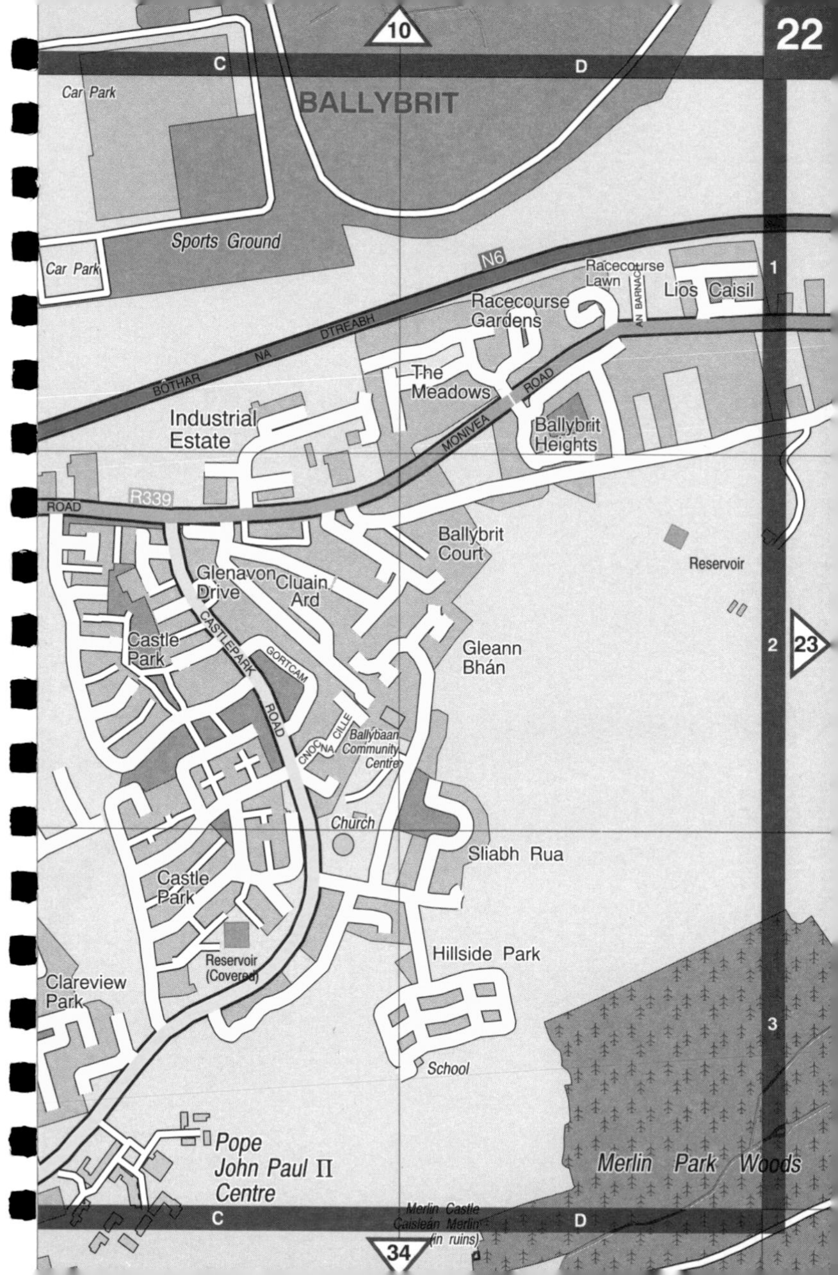
10
C
D
BALLYBRIT
Car Park
Sports Ground
Car Park
N6
BÓTHAR NA DTREABH
Racecourse Lawn
AN BARNAC
Lios Caisil
1
Racecourse Gardens
The Meadows
MONIVEA ROAD
Ballybrit Heights
Industrial Estate
R339
ROAD
Ballybrit Court
Reservoir
Glenavon Drive
Cluain Ard
CASTLEPARK ROAD
GORTCAM
Castle Park
Gleann Bhán
2
23
CNOC NA CILLE
Ballybaan Community Centre
Church
Sliabh Rua
Castle Park
Reservoir (Covered)
Hillside Park
Clareview Park
School
3
Pope John Paul II Centre
Merlin Park Woods
Merlin Castle
Caisleán Merlin
(in ruins)
C
D
34

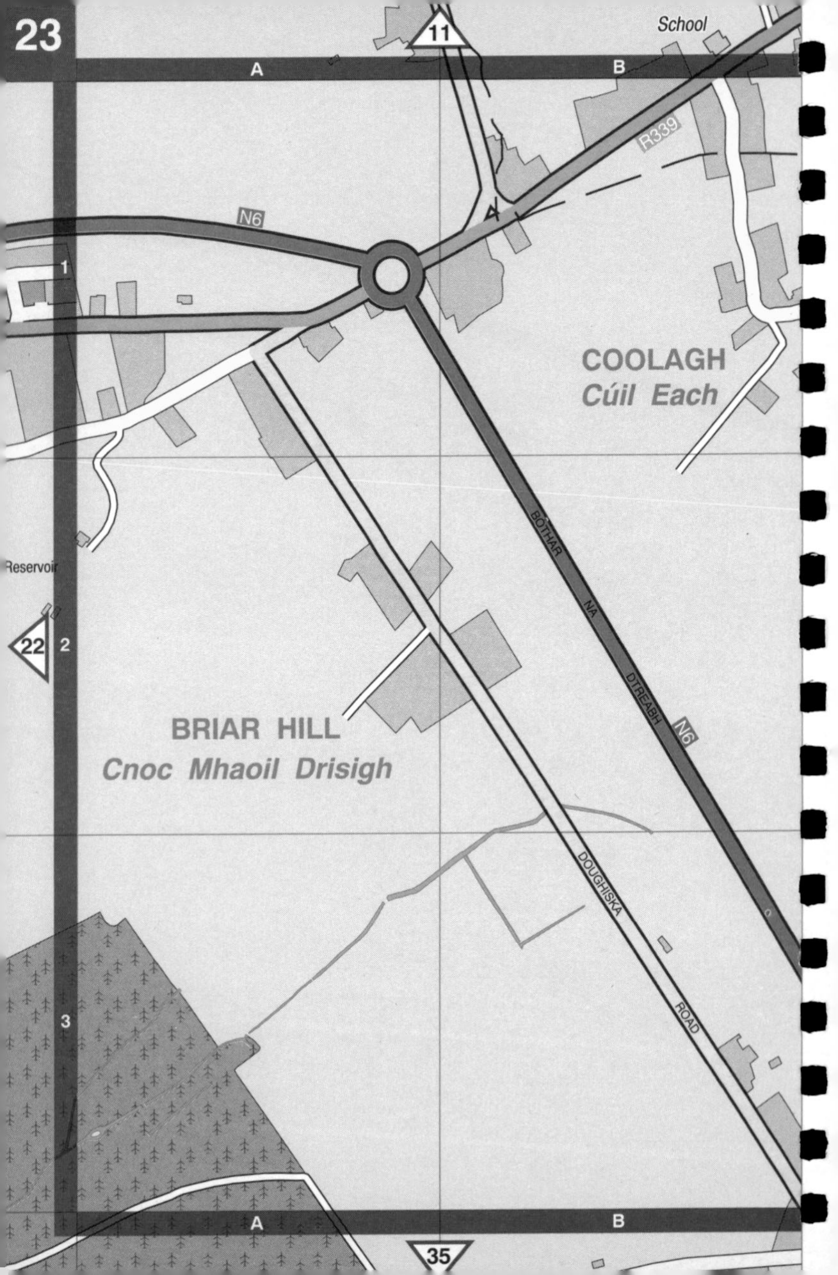
11
School
A
B
R339
N6
1
COOLAGH
Cúil Each
BOTHAR
NA
DTREABH
N6
Reservoir
22
2
BRIAR HILL
Cnoc Mhaoil Drisigh
DOUGHISKA
ROAD
3
A
B
35

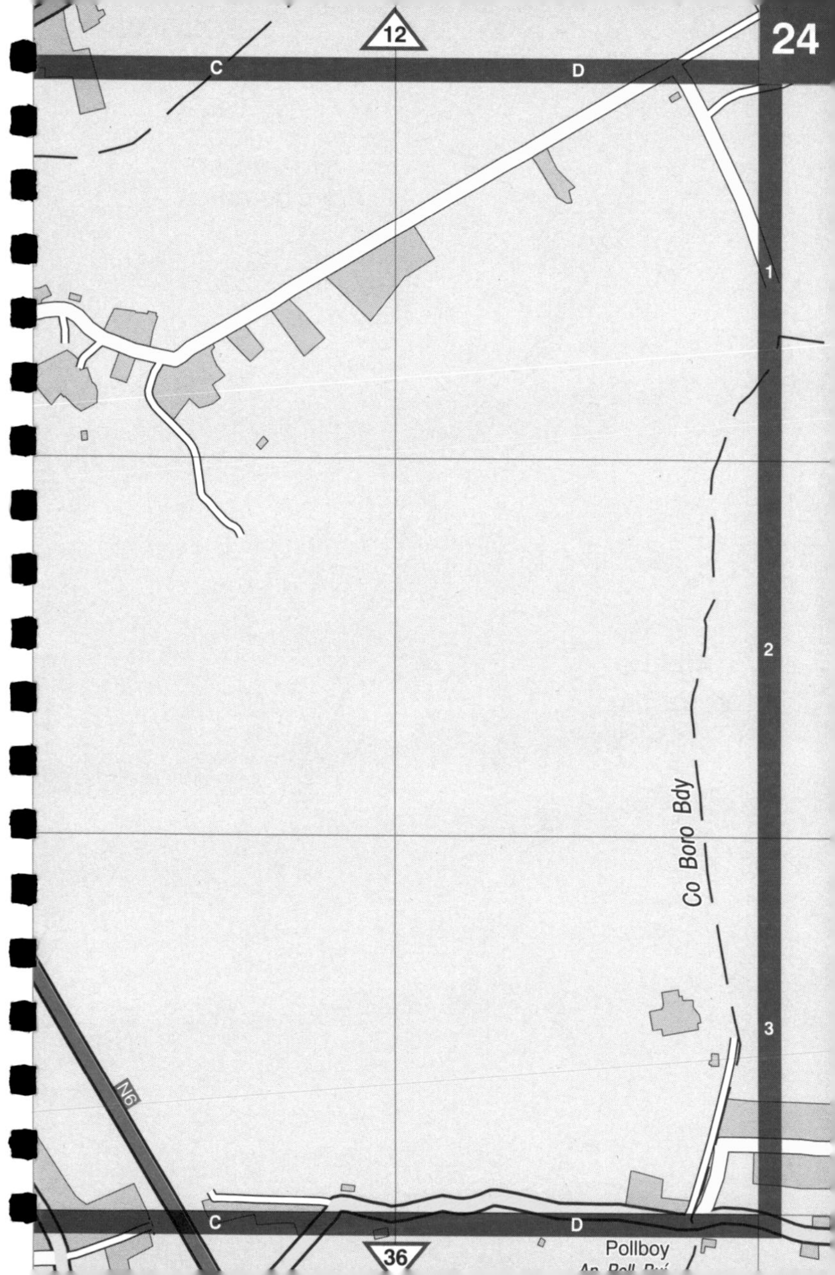
12
C
D
1
2
3
Co Boro Bdy
N6
C
D
36
Pollboy

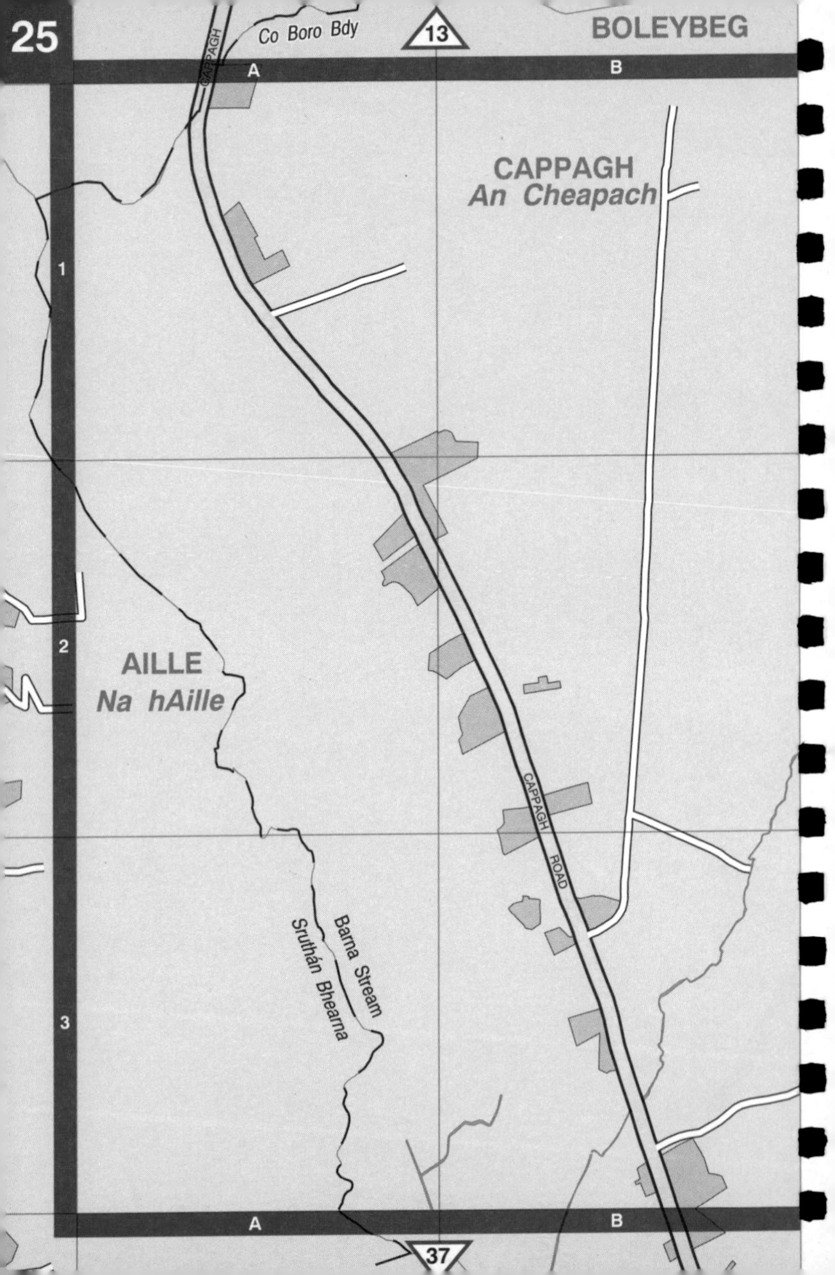
Co Boro Bdy
13
BOLEYBEG
A
B
CAPPAGH
CAPPAGH
An Cheapach
1
2
AILLE
Na hAille
CAPPAGH
ROAD
3
Barna Stream
Sruthán Bhearna
A
B
37

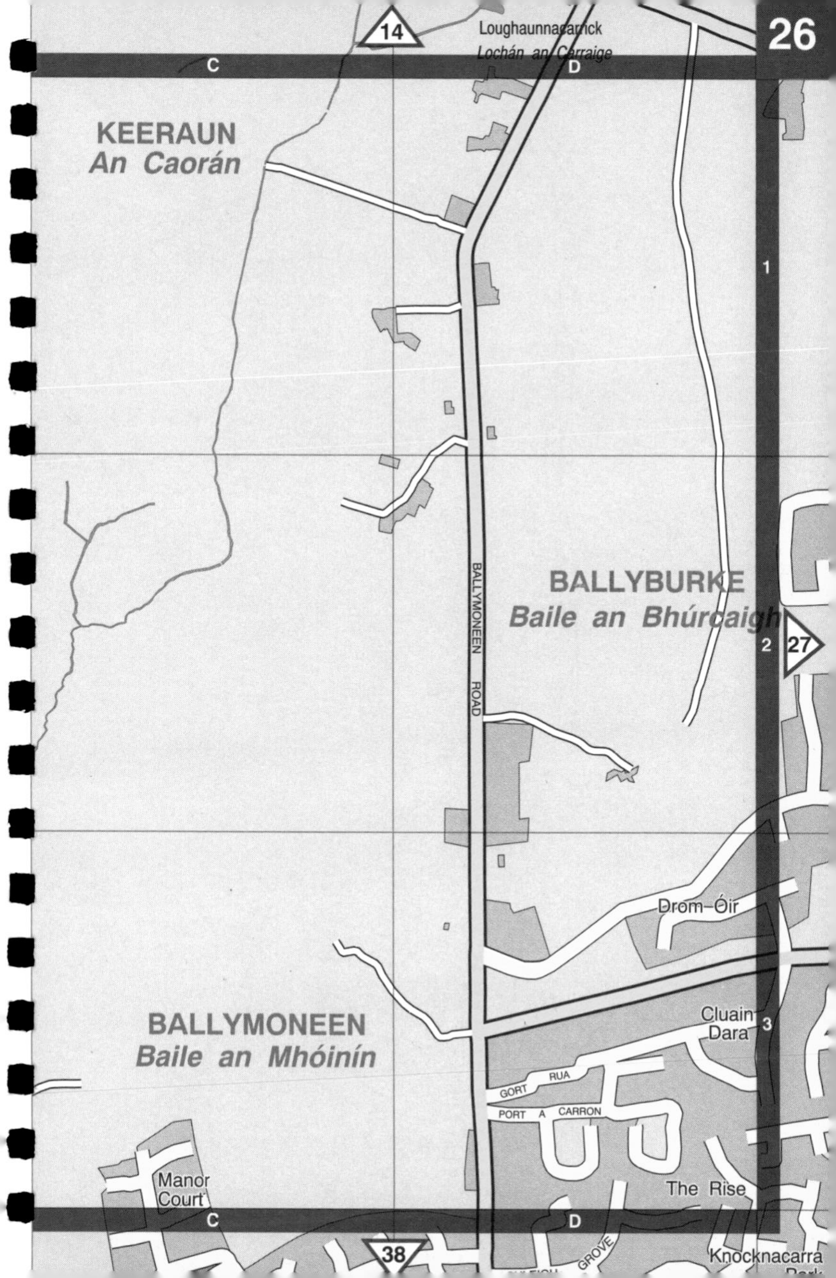
14
Loughaunnacarrick
Lochán an Carraige
C
D
KEERAUN
An Caorán
1
BALLYMONEEN ROAD
BALLYBURKE
Baile an Bhúrcaigh
2
27
Drom-Óir
Cluain Dara
3
GORT RUA
PORT A CARRON
BALLYMONEEN
Baile an Mhóinín
Manor Court
The Rise
C
D
38
GROVE
Knocknacarra

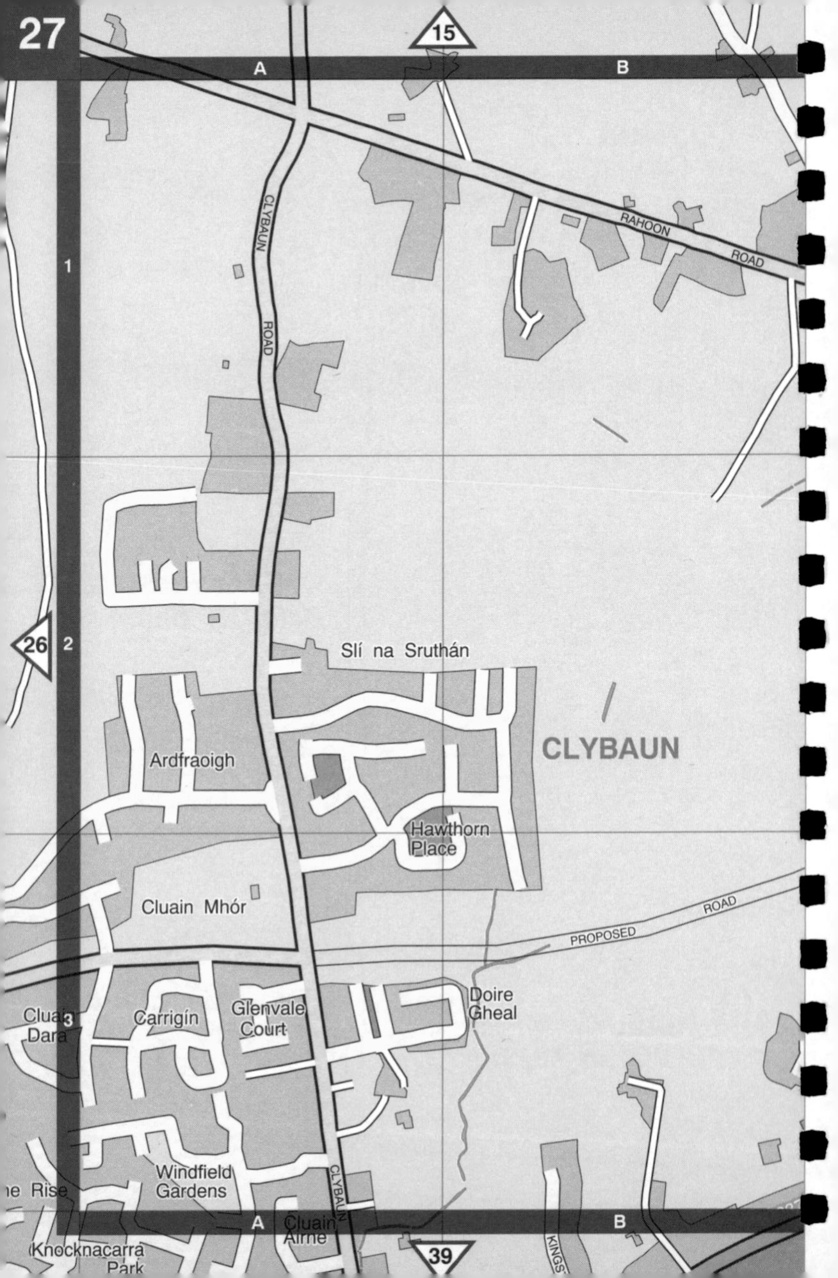
15
A
B
RAHOON
ROAD
CLYBAUN
ROAD
1
26
2
Slí na Sruthán
CLYBAUN
Ardfraoigh
Hawthorn
Place
Cluain Mhór
PROPOSED
ROAD
Doire
Gheal
Cluain
Dara
3
Carrigín
Glenvale
Court
Windfield
Gardens
he Rise
CLYBAUN
A
Cluain
Airne
B
Knocknacarra
Park
KINGS
39

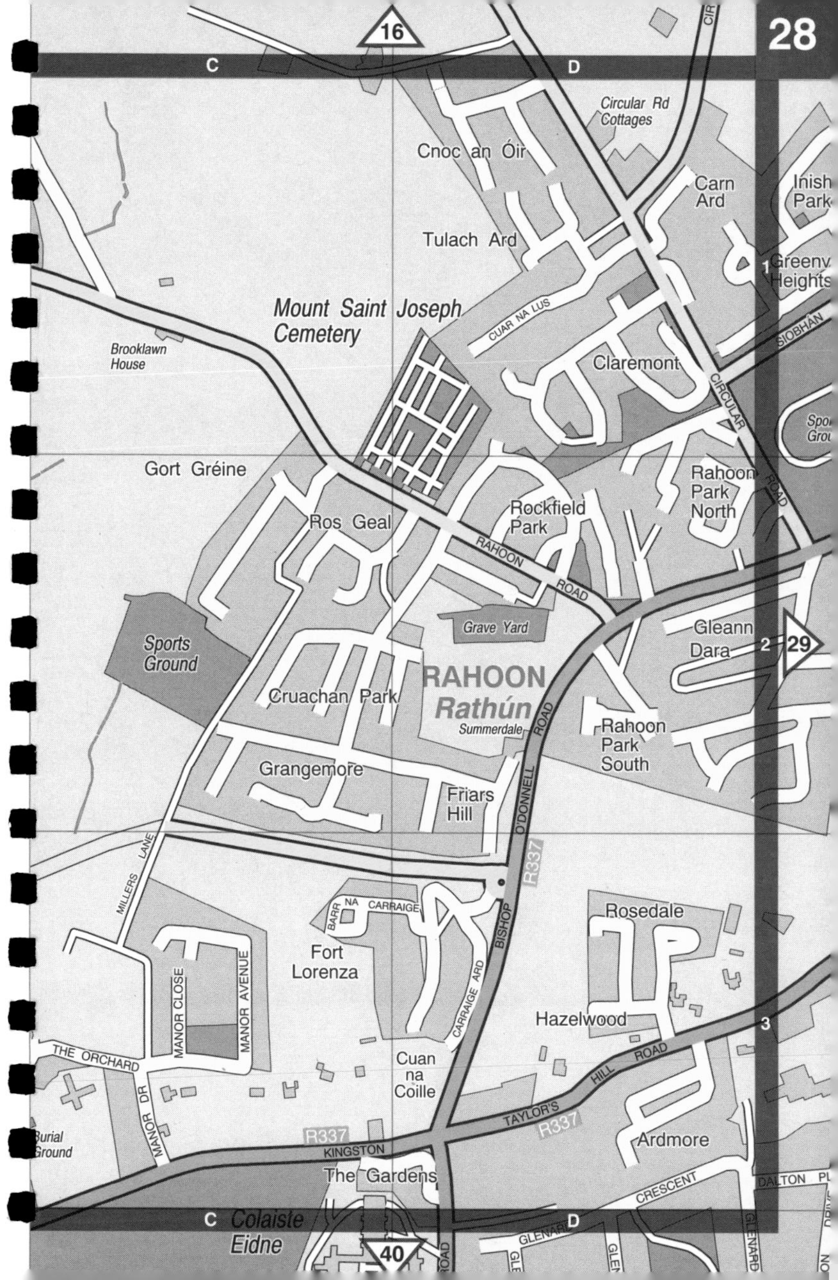
16
C
D
Circular Rd Cottages
Cnoc an Óir
Carn Ard
Inish Park
Tulach Ard
1
Greenv Heights
Mount Saint Joseph Cemetery
CUAR NA LUS
SIOBHÁN
Brooklawn House
Claremont
CIRCULAR ROAD
Gort Gréine
Rahoon Park North
Rockfield Park
Ros Geal
RAHOON ROAD
Grave Yard
Gleann Dara
2
29
Sports Ground
RAHOON
Rathún
Cruachan Park
Summerdale
Rahoon Park South
Grangemore
O'DONNELL ROAD
Friars Hill
MILLERS LANE
R337
BARR NA CARRAIGE
Rosedale
BISHOP
Fort Lorenza
MANOR CLOSE
MANOR AVENUE
CARRAIGE ARD
Hazelwood
3
THE ORCHARD
Cuan na Coille
HILL ROAD
TAYLOR'S
MANOR DR
Burial Ground
Ardmore
KINGSTON
The Gardens
CRESCENT
DALTON PL
C
Colaiste Eidne
D
GLENARD
40

17
A
B
Gaelcarraig Park
John Coogan Park
Carn Ard
Inishannagh Park
Camillaun Park
Greenview Heights
Westside Community Centre
Shopping Centre
Church
UNIVERSITY COLLEGE HOSPITAL
SIOBHÁN McKENNA ROAD
BÓTHAR LE CHÉILE
CARBRY RD
SEAMUS
Sports Ground
CIRCULAR ROAD
SEAMUS QUIRKE ROAD
R338
Rahoon Park North
ASH ROAD
SHANTALLOW
COSTELLO
DAVIS ROAD
COLMCILLE ROAD
FURSEY ROAD
Mc DARA ROAD
O'FLAHERTY RD
BÓTHAR UÍ ROIDEACHÁIN
SEAMUS QUIRKE ROAD
MOUNT PLEASANT DRIVE
School
Conv
RAHOON ROAD
SHANTALLA ROAD
BÓTHAR PHADRAIC UÍ CHONNAIRE
28
2
1
OAKLEY CRES
ROCKMOUNT ROAD
AVONDALE ROAD
SYCAMORE DRIVE
BEECHMOUNT ROAD
CEDARWOOD CLOSE
NEW AVENUE
SHANTALLA PLACE
Spire Gardens
Sports Ground
School
Chapel
ARDMORE ROAD
Highfield Park
MAUNSELLS PARK
MAUNSELLS ROAD
ASHDALE ROAD
BEECHMOUNT AVENUE
RIVENDELL
Ard na Coille
The Nurseries
Averard West
ST MARY'S PARK
R337
TAYLOR'S HILL ROAD
3
Conv
Sch
ROSARY LANE
Tennis Ground
St Mary's Ter
Suncroft Court
ST MARY'S AVE
Sports Ground
KYLEMORE PARK
SALTHILL ROAD
R864
St Josephs Tce
DEVON CT
DALTON PL
DRIVE
DEVON MEWS
DEVON GARDENS
Devon Park
WHITESTRAND
Churchfields
The Maples
GLENARD
41
Rosmeen Court

18
C
D
Church
CORRIB RIVER CRUISES
Eglinton Pier
Slipway
Boat Club
Water Works
Sports Ground
Lock
Salmon Weir
Riverside Sports Ground
Rowing Club
Weir
UNIVERSITY ROAD
Chapel
Social Science Centre
Beggars Bridge
Town Hall
Theatre
Rehab Inst
Court Ho
COURTHOUSE SQUARE
ST VINCENT'S AVE
Sports Ground
Salmon Weir Br
POTATO MARKET
ST NICHOLAS'S CATHEDRAL
Monastery
Burial Gd
Abbey
Health Centre
Chap
GPO
Nun's Island
King's Gap
Oakwood Close
Lynch's Castle
Nora Barnacle House
Lynch's Window
St Mary's College
Maderia Court
Monastery
William O'Brien Bridge
Theatre
Library
Custom Ho
Fish Market
SPANISH PARADE
Spanish Arch
Museum
Wolfe Tone Bridge
Sports Ground
Hall
Fire Sta
Fr Burke Park
Grave Yd
Priory
Ballyknow Quay
Crescent Green
Lios Ealtan
Hall
NIMMO'S PIER
Grattan Court
Grattan Park
Whitestrand
42
CLADDAGH
An Cladagh
31
1
2
3

TOWNPARKS
Shopping Centre
19
New Cemetery
Coole Park
Sports Ground
Greyhound Racing Track
Sports Ground
James Connolly Terrace
Cabbage La
Cill Ard
Bohermore
Blake's Lane
Water Lane
R866
Headford Road
Dyke Road
Cinema
Slipway
Riverside Sports Ground
Walsh's Ter
St Bridget's
St Bridget's Place Upper
St Bridget's Pl
St Bridget's Ter
R336
Forster Court
The Green
Glenmore
Grammer Sch
City Hall
College Road
R339
County Buildings
Brendan's Avenue
Bóthar na mBan
Prospect Hill
Bóthar Uí Eithir
Bóthar Irwin
Tax Office
Potato Market
Wood Qy
Eyre St
Ch
Hall
Conv
Chapel
Forster Street
St Augustine's Well
Lough Atalia
St Mary Magdalen's Ter
Fair Green
The Elms
St Patrick's Ave
Rosemary Ave
Town Wall
Browne Doorway
Toilets
Kennedy Park
Eyre Square
Williamsgate St
Eglinton St
GPO
Daly's Pl
Frenchville Lane
Abattoir
Station Rd
Ceannt Station
Ball Alley Lane
William St
Castle Street
Tourist Office
Victoria Pl
Queen Street
30
Abbeygate St
Whitehall
Lwr Road
St Augustine St
Middle St
Theatre
Merchants Road
Oil Depot
Forthill Grave Yd
Atalia Road
Lough Atalia Road
Dock Road
Mooring Posts
Commercial Dock
Dún Aengus Dock
Dock Street
The Long Walk
Old Dock
Departure Point Aran Island Ferry
New Pier
New Dock St
Custom Ho
Libra
An Rinn Mhór
Rinmore Point
Nimmo's Pier
Mooring Posts
A
B
1
2
3

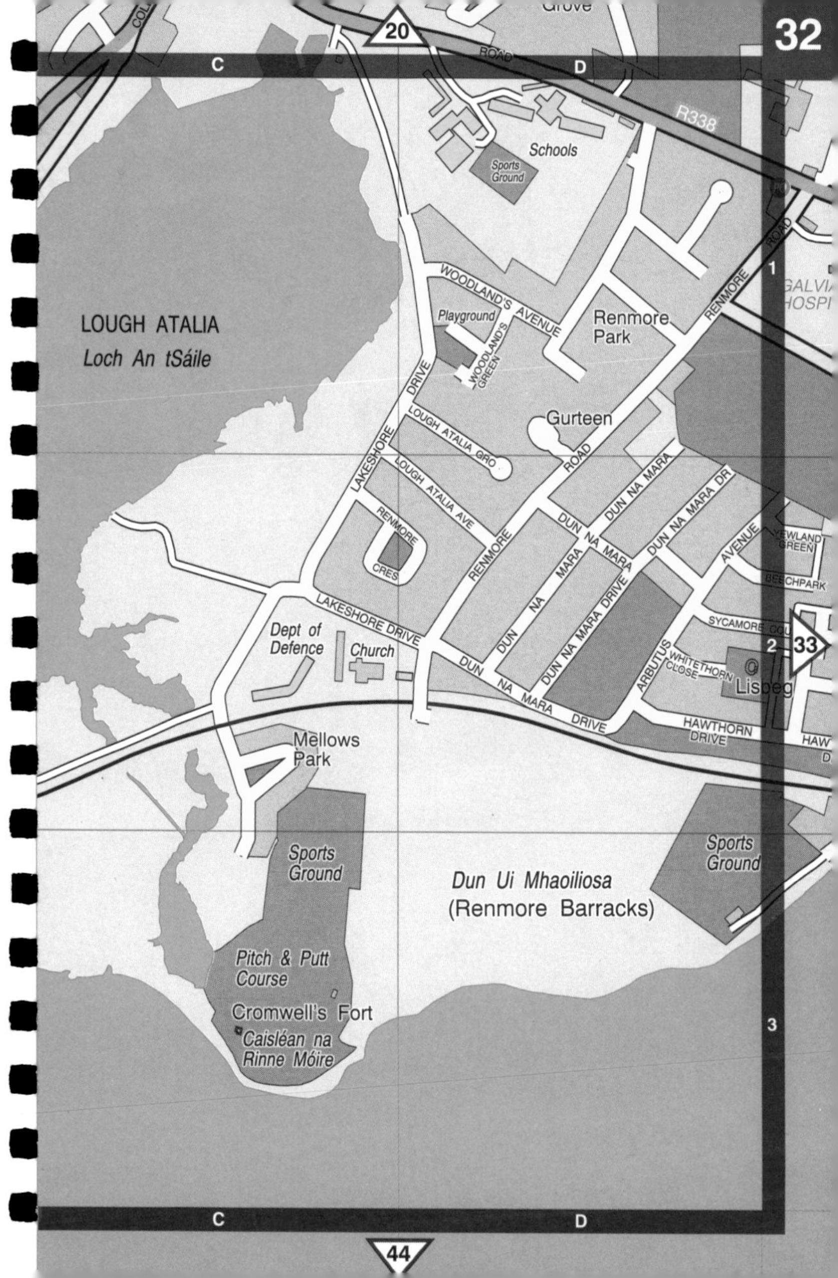
20
C
D
ROAD
R338
Schools
Sports Ground
WOODLAND'S AVENUE
Playground
WOODLAND'S GREEN
Renmore Park
RENMORE ROAD
1
LOUGH ATALIA
Loch An tSáile
LAKESHORE DRIVE
LOUGH ATALIA GRO
Gurteen
LOUGH ATALIA AVE
RENMORE CRES
DUN NA MARA
DUN NA MARA DR
AVENUE
YEWLAND GREEN
BEECHPARK
SYCAMORE COU
LAKESHORE DRIVE
Dept of Defence
Church
DUN NA MARA DRIVE
ARBUTUS
WHITETHORN CLOSE
Lisbeg
2
33
HAWTHORN DRIVE
Mellows Park
Sports Ground
Dun Ui Mhaoiliosa
(Renmore Barracks)
Sports Ground
Pitch & Putt Course
Cromwell's Fort
Caisléan na Rinne Móire
3
C
D
44

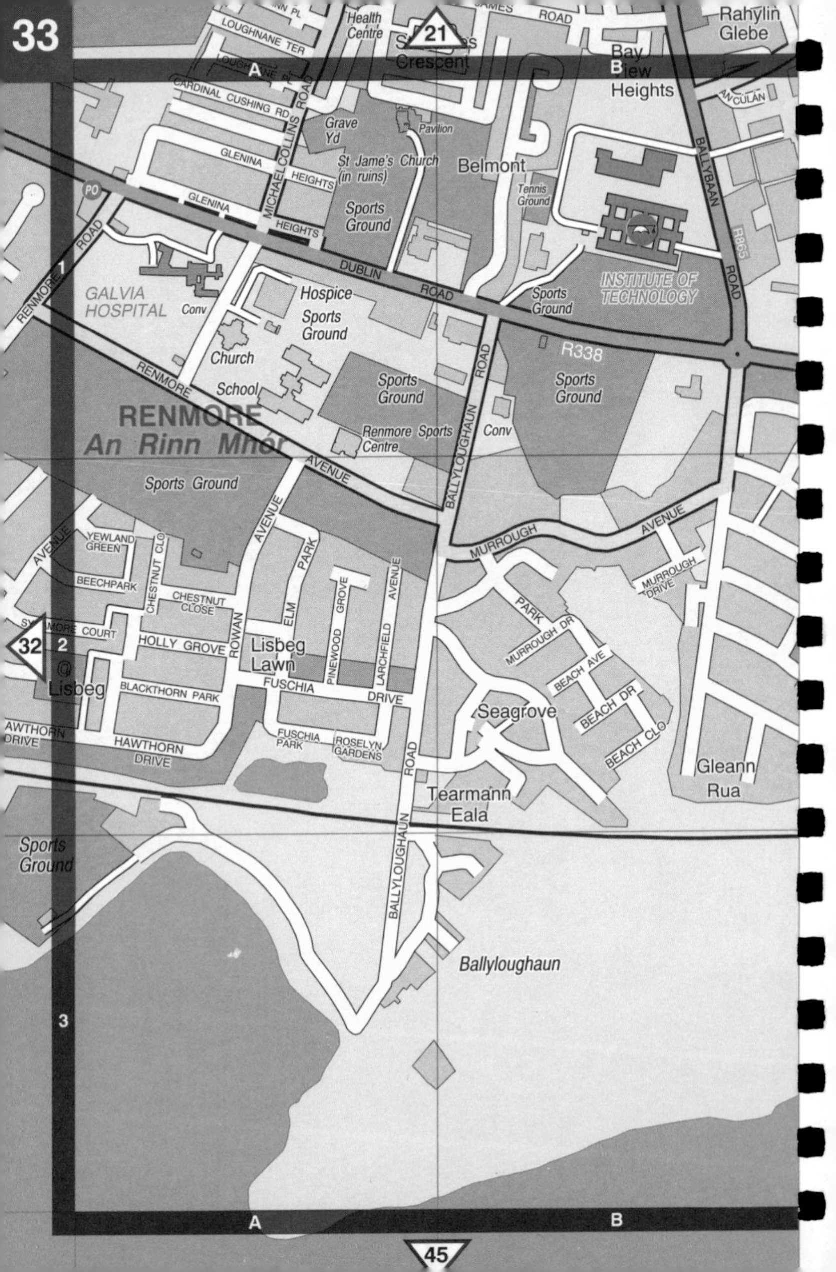
Rahylin Glebe
Health Centre
21
St James's Crescent
Bay View Heights
LOUGHNANE TER
CARDINAL CUSHING RD
MICHAEL COLLINS ROAD
Grave Yd
Pavilion
St James's Church (in ruins)
Belmont
GLENINA
HEIGHTS
Sports Ground
Tennis Ground
BALLYBAAN ROAD
R865
AN CULAN
PO
RENMORE ROAD
DUBLIN ROAD
INSTITUTE OF TECHNOLOGY
GALVIA HOSPITAL
Conv
Hospice
Church
School
R338
RENMORE AVENUE
BALLYLOUGHAUN ROAD
RENMORE
An Rinn Mhór
Renmore Sports Centre
MURROUGH AVENUE
YEWLAND GREEN
BEECHPARK
CHESTNUT CLO
CHESTNUT CLOSE
ROWAN AVENUE
ELM PARK
PINEWOOD GROVE
LARCHFIELD AVENUE
MURROUGH DRIVE
PARK
MURROUGH DR
BEACH AVE
BEACH DR
BEACH CLO
SYCAMORE COURT
32
HOLLY GROVE
Lisbeg Lawn
Lisbeg
BLACKTHORN PARK
FUSCHIA DRIVE
HAWTHORN DRIVE
FUSCHIA PARK
ROSELYN GARDENS
Seagrove
Gleann Rua
Tearmann Eala
Ballyloughaun
A
B
1
2
3
45

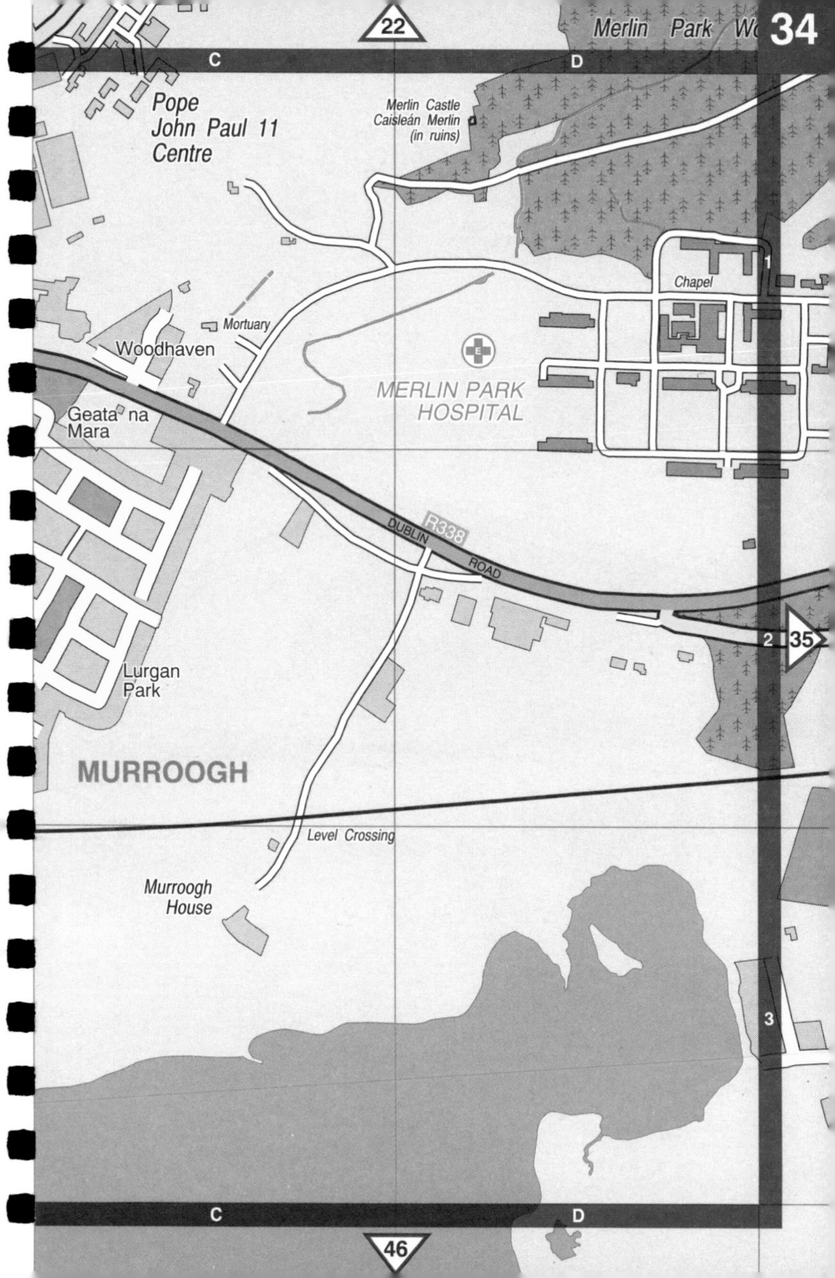
22
Merlin Park Wo
C
D
Pope
John Paul 11
Centre
Merlin Castle
Caisleán Merlin
(in ruins)
1
Chapel
Mortuary
Woodhaven
E
MERLIN PARK
HOSPITAL
Geata na
Mara
R338
DUBLIN
ROAD
2
35
Lurgan
Park
MURROOGH
Level Crossing
Murroogh
House
3
C
D
46

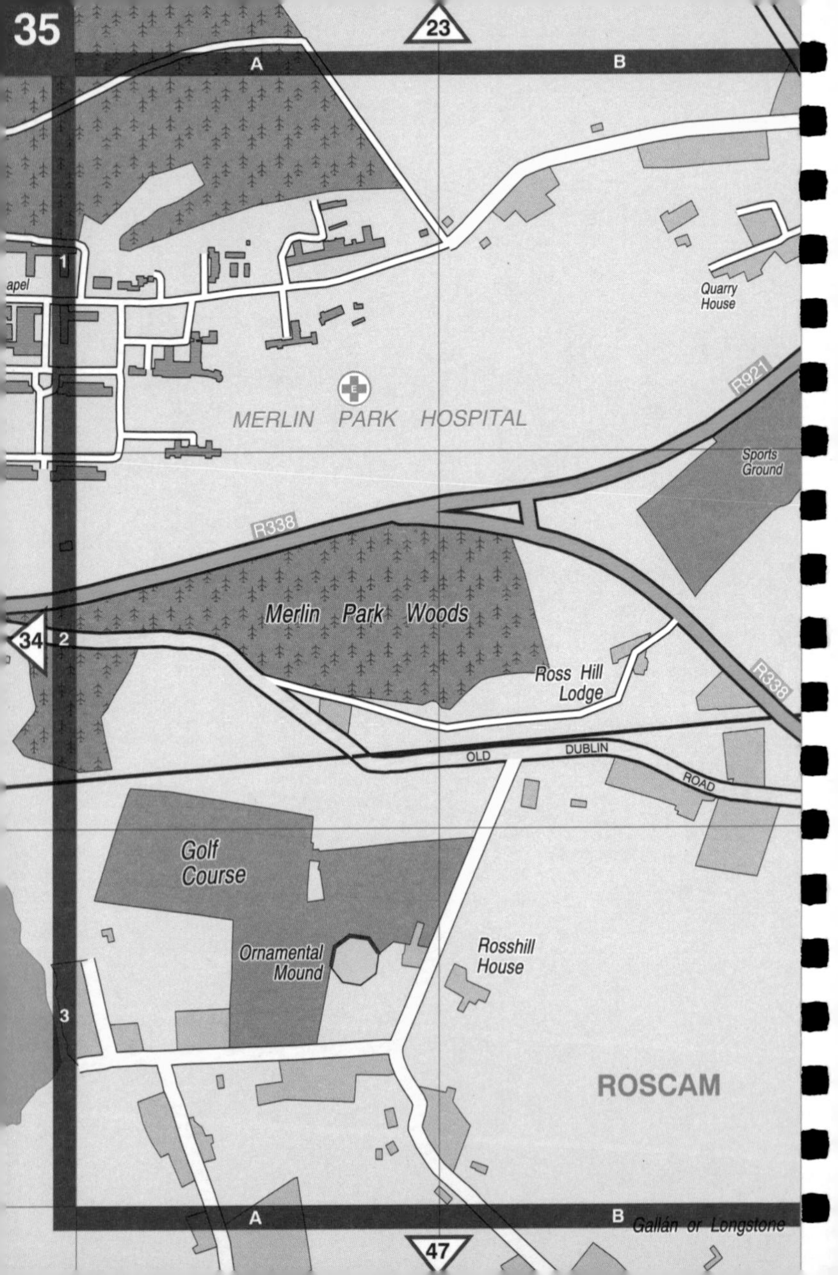
23
A
B
1
apel
Quarry House
R921
MERLIN PARK HOSPITAL
Sports Ground
R338
Merlin Park Woods
34
2
Ross Hill Lodge
R338
OLD DUBLIN ROAD
Golf Course
Ornamental Mound
Rosshill House
3
ROSCAM
A
B
Gallán or Longstone
47

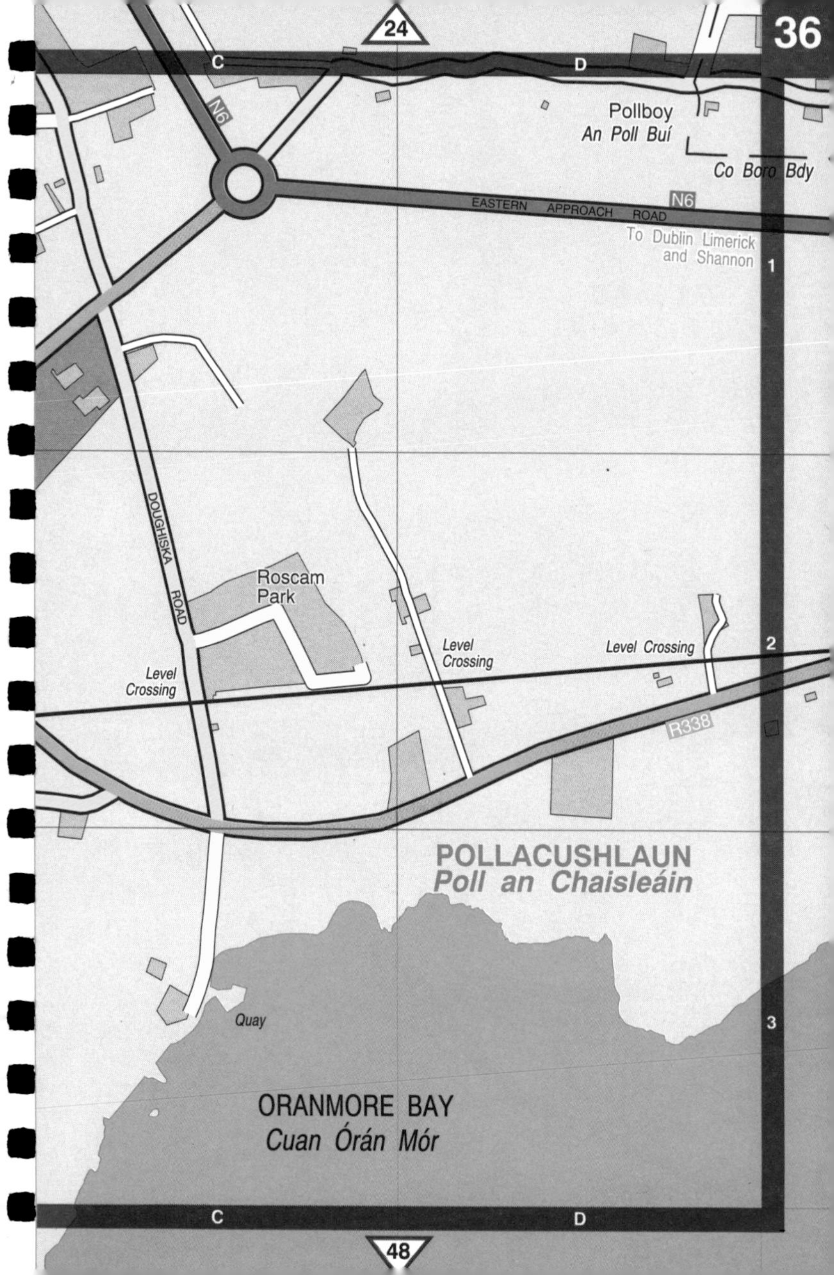
24
C
D
N6
Pollboy
An Poll Buí
Co Boro Bdy
EASTERN APPROACH ROAD
N6
To Dublin Limerick and Shannon
1
DOUGHISKA ROAD
Roscam Park
Level Crossing
Level Crossing
Level Crossing
2
R338
POLLACUSHLAUN
Poll an Chaisleáin
Quay
3
ORANMORE BAY
Cuan Órán Mór
C
D
48

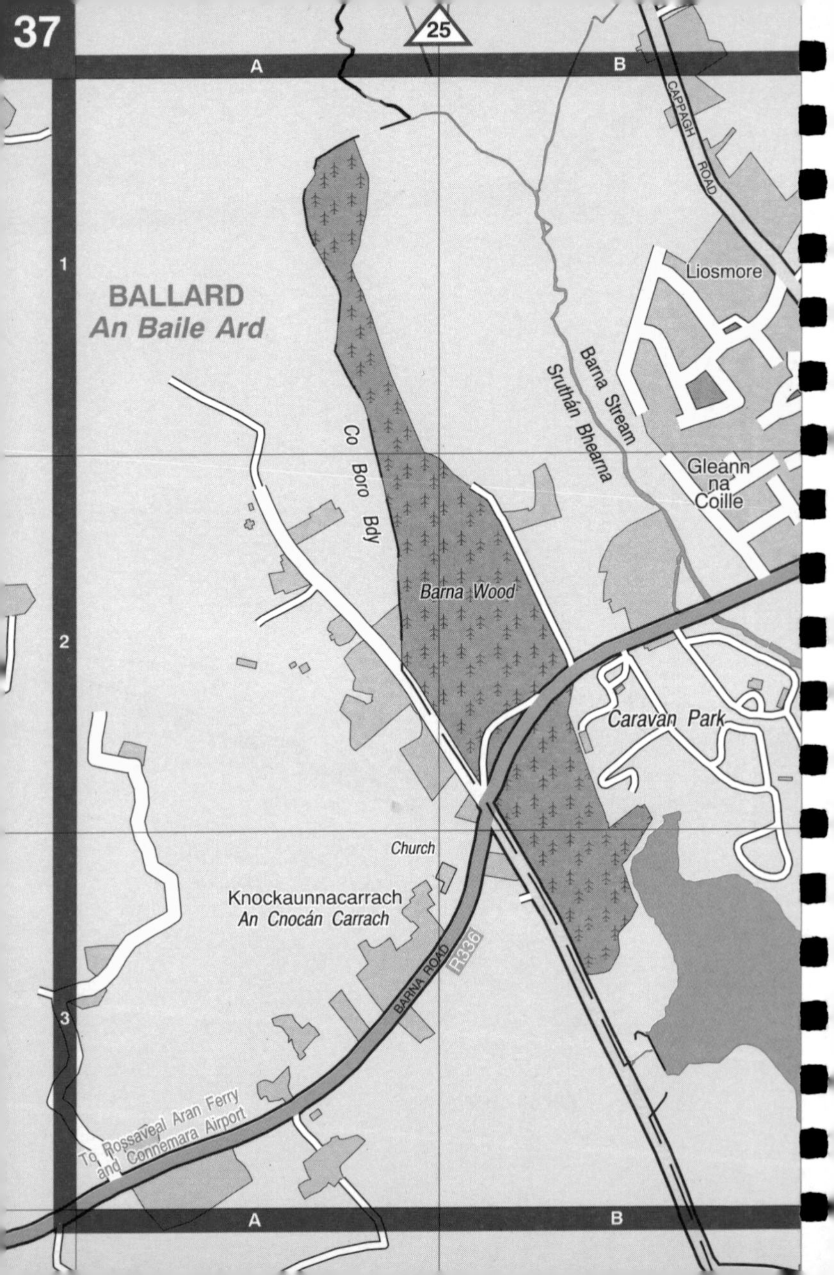
25
A
B
CAPPAGH ROAD
Liosmore
1
BALLARD
An Baile Ard
Barna Stream
Sruthán Bhearna
Co Boro Bdy
Gleann na Coille
Barna Wood
2
Caravan Park
Church
Knockaunnacarrach
An Cnocán Carrach
BARNA ROAD
R336
3
To Rossaveal Aran Ferry and Connemara Airport
A
B

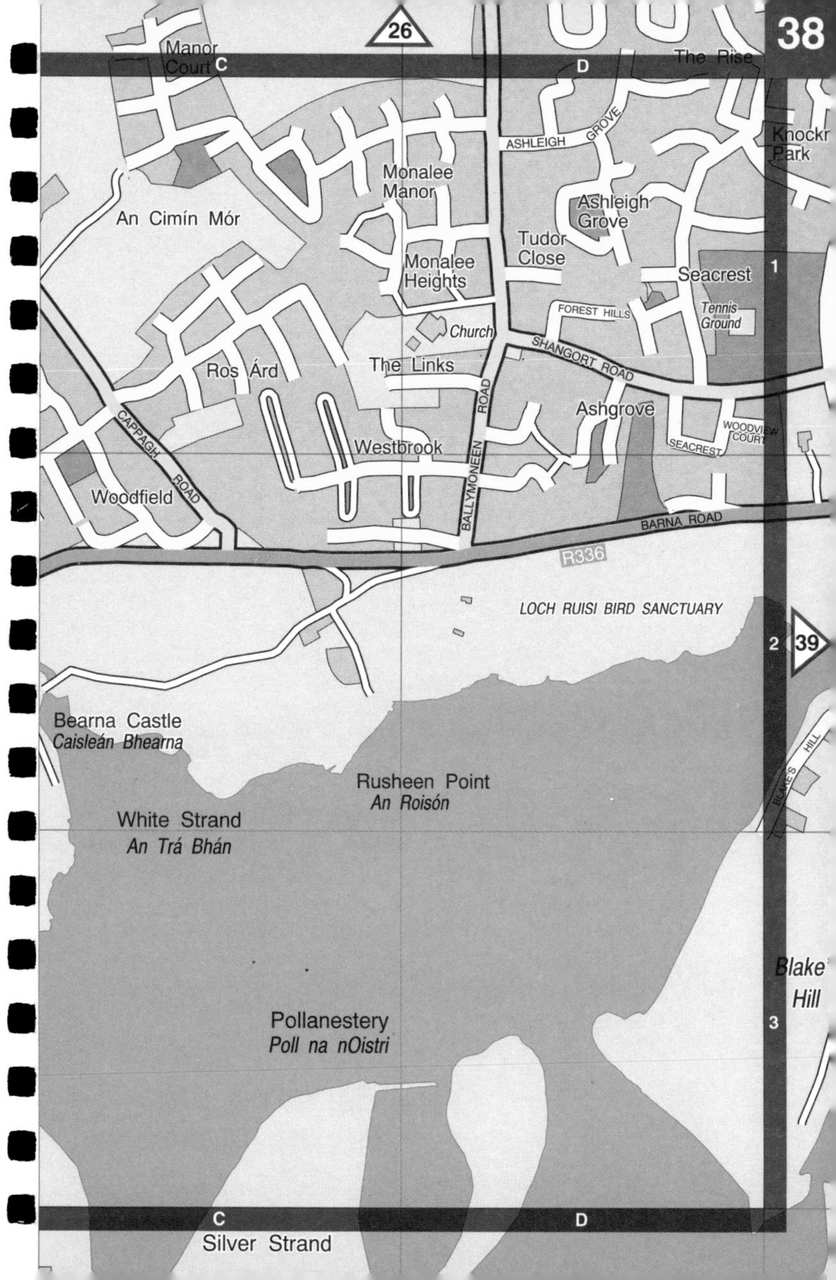
26
Manor Court
C
D
The Rise
Knockr Park
ASHLEIGH GROVE
Monalee Manor
An Cimín Mór
Ashleigh Grove
Tudor Close
Monalee Heights
Seacrest
1
FOREST HILLS
Tennis Ground
Church
SHANGORT ROAD
Ros Árd
The Links
Ashgrove
BALLYMONEEN ROAD
CAPPAGH ROAD
WOODVIEW COURT
SEACREST
Westbrook
Woodfield
BARNA ROAD
R336
LOCH RUISI BIRD SANCTUARY
2
39
Bearna Castle
Caisleán Bhearna
BLAKE'S HILL
Rusheen Point
An Roisón
White Strand
An Trá Bhán
Blake'
Hill
Pollanestery
Poll na nOistri
3
C
D
Silver Strand

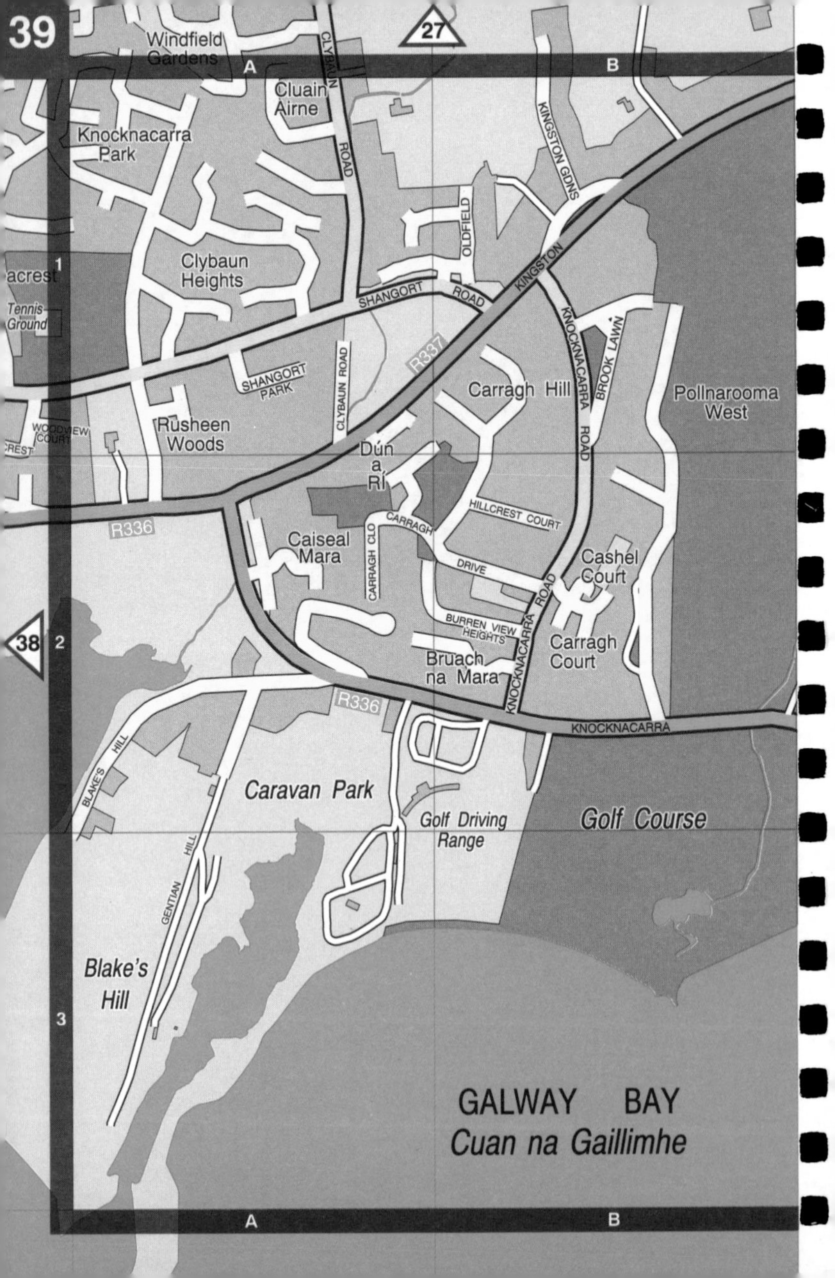
27
A
B
Windfield Gardens
Cluain Airne
CLYBAUN ROAD
Knocknacarra Park
KINGSTON GDNS
OLDFIELD
Clybaun Heights
acrest
Tennis Ground
1
SHANGORT ROAD
KINGSTON
KNOCKNACARRA ROAD
BROOK LAWN
R337
SHANGORT PARK
CLYBAUN ROAD
Carragh Hill
Pollnarooma West
Rusheen Woods
WOODVIEW COURT
CREST
Dún a Rí
HILLCREST COURT
R336
CARRAGH
Caiseal Mara
CARRAGH CLO
DRIVE
Cashel Court
BURREN VIEW HEIGHTS
38
2
Carragh Court
Bruach na Mara
KNOCKNACARRA ROAD
R336
KNOCKNACARRA
BLAKE'S HILL
Caravan Park
Golf Driving Range
Golf Course
GENTIAN HILL
Blake's Hill
3
GALWAY BAY
Cuan na Gaillimhe
A
B

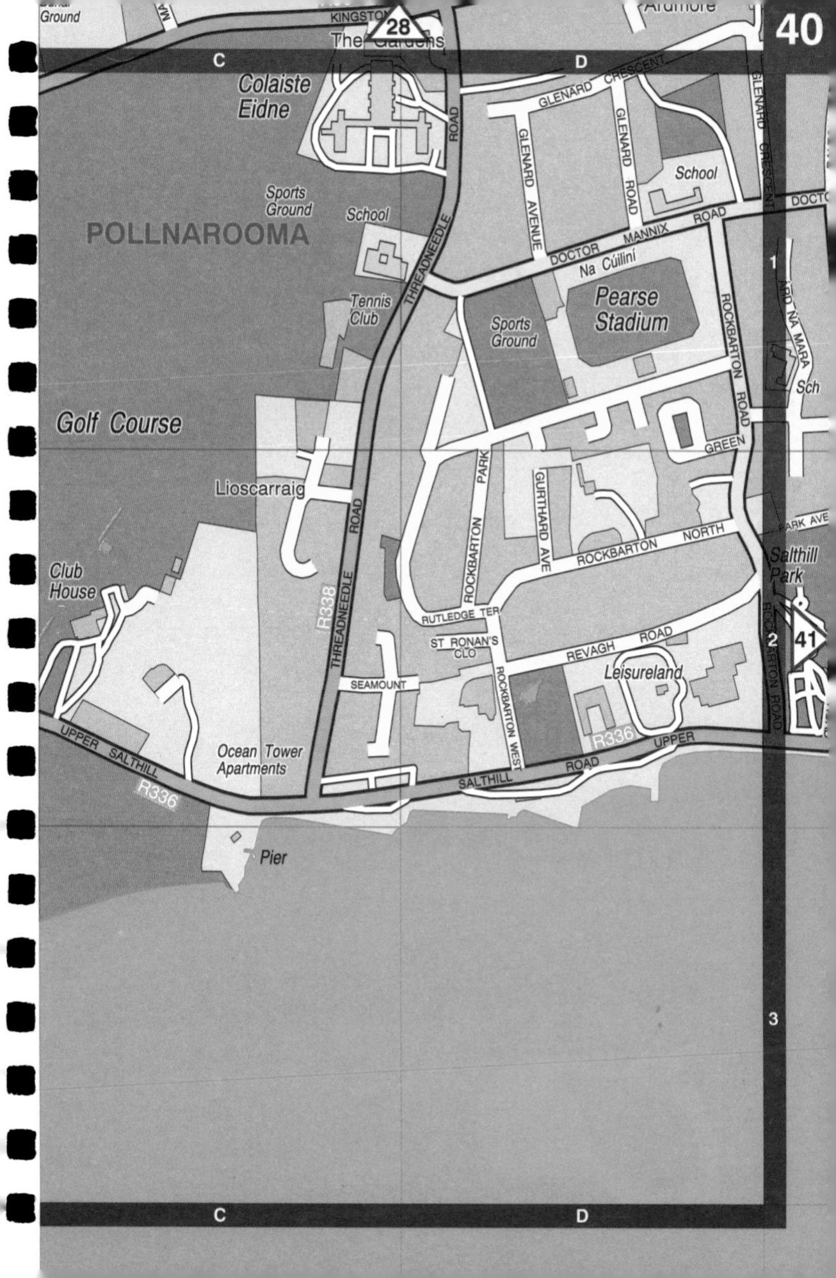
Ground
KINGSTON
28
The Gardens
Ardmore
C
D
Colaiste
Eidne
THREADNEEDLE ROAD
GLENARD CRESCENT
GLENARD AVENUE
GLENARD ROAD
School
DOCTOR MANNIX ROAD
Na Cúilíní
Sports
Ground
School
POLLNAROOMA
Tennis
Club
Sports
Ground
Pearse
Stadium
ROCKBARTON ROAD
ÁRD NA MARA
Sch
Golf Course
GREEN
Lioscarraig
ROCKBARTON PARK
GURTHARD AVE
PARK AVE
ROCKBARTON NORTH
Salthill
Park
Club
House
R338
RUTLEDGE TER
ST RONAN'S
CLO
REVAGH ROAD
41
Leisureland
SEAMOUNT
ROCKBARTON WEST
R336
UPPER SALTHILL ROAD
Ocean Tower
Apartments
R336
Pier
1
2
3
C
D

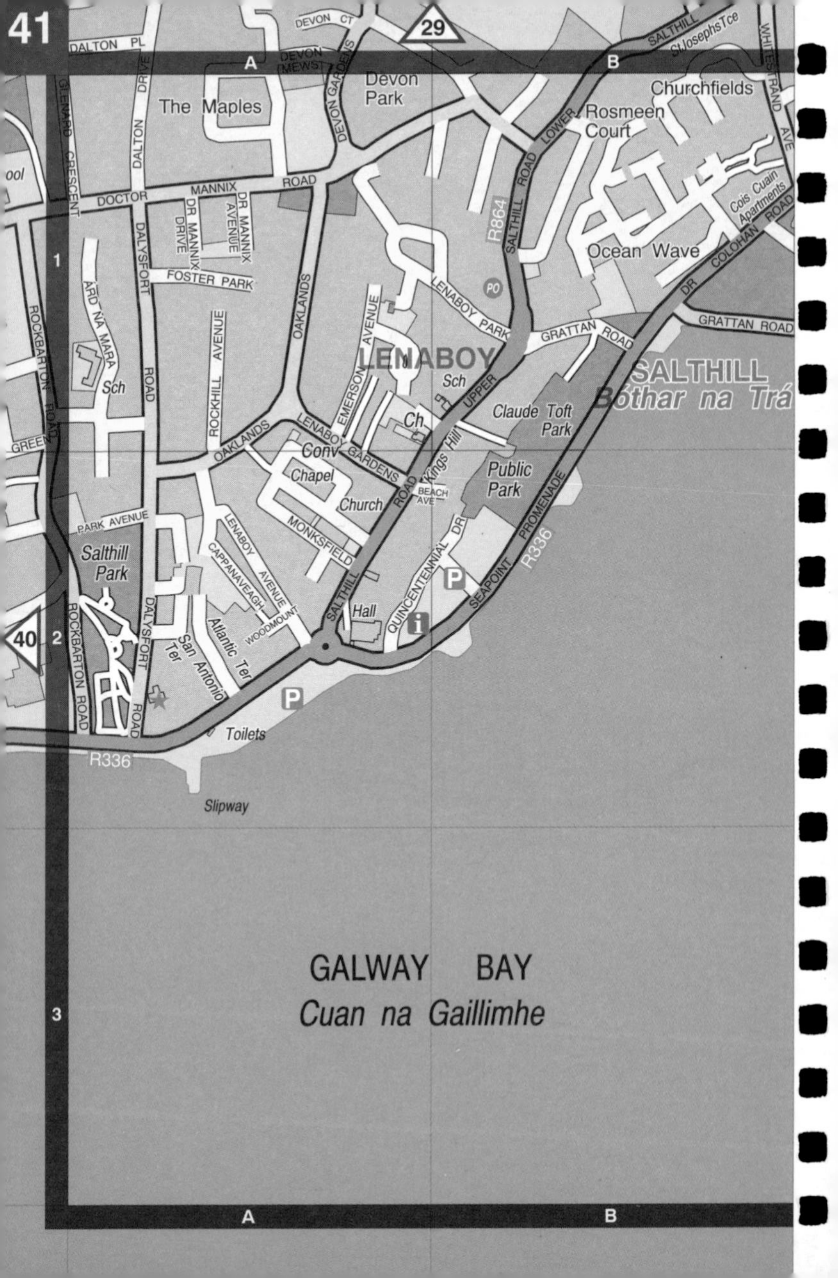
29
40
A
B
1
2
3
DALTON PL
DEVON CT
DEVON MEWS
DEVON GARDENS
Devon Park
The Maples
GLENARD CRESCENT
DALTON DRIVE
SALTHILL
St.JosephsTce
WHITESTRAND AVE
Churchfields
Rosmeen Court
LOWER
SALTHILL ROAD
R864
DOCTOR MANNIX ROAD
DR MANNIX DRIVE
DR MANNIX AVENUE
FOSTER PARK
Cois Cuain Apartments
Ocean Wave
DR COLOHAN ROAD
GRATTAN ROAD
LENABOY PARK
PO
ÁRD NA MARA
ROCKBARTON ROAD
DALYSFORT ROAD
ROCKHILL AVENUE
OAKLANDS
EMERSON AVENUE
LENABOY
Sch
SALTHILL
Bóthar na Trá
UPPER
Claude Toft Park
Ch
Kings Hill
LENABOY GARDENS
Conv
Chapel
Church
GREEN
BEACH AVE
Public Park
PROMENADE
PARK AVENUE
MONKSFIELD
QUINCENTENNIAL DR
R336
Salthill Park
LENABOY AVENUE
CAPPANAVEAGH
SEAPOINT
P
Hall
WOODMOUNT
i
Atlantic Ter
San Antonio Ter
ROCKBARTON ROAD
Toilets
Slipway
GALWAY BAY
Cuan na Gaillimhe

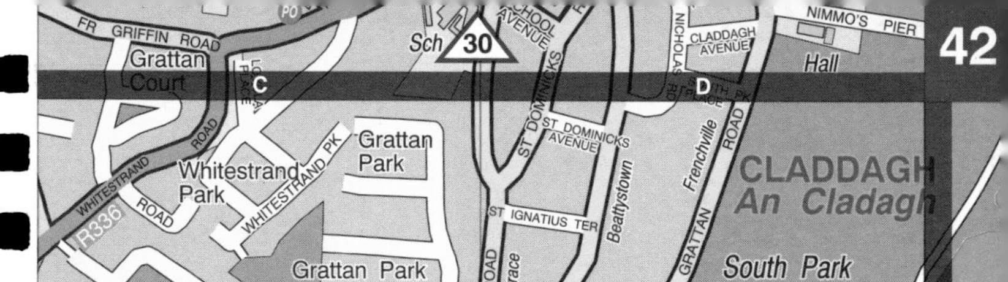

1

43

2

MUTTON ISLAND

Oileán Caorach

3

C

D

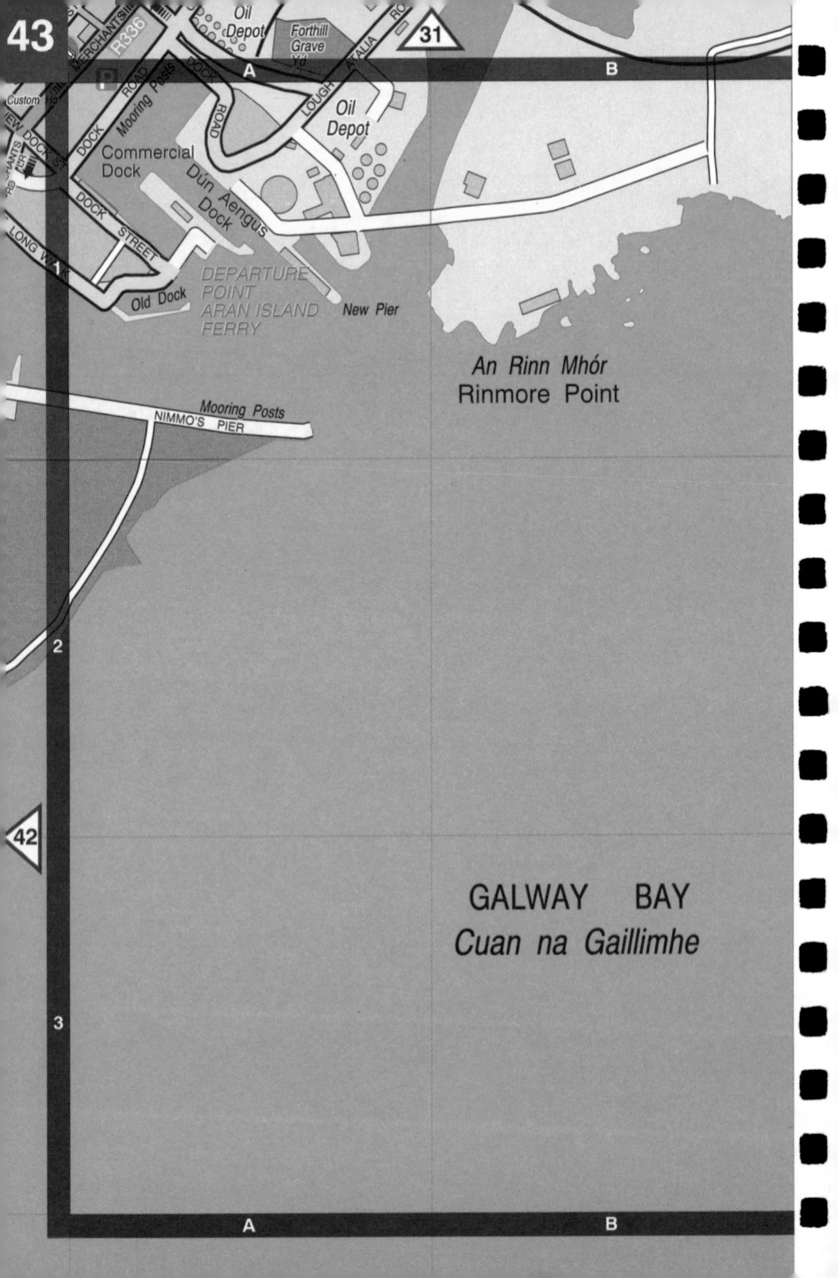
31
A
B
Oil
Depot
Forthill
Grave
Yd
MERCHANTS
R336
DOCK
ROAD
LOUGH
ATALIA
Custom Ho
Mooring Posts
Oil
Depot
Commercial
Dock
Dún Aengus
Dock
DOCK
STREET
LONG WALK
NEW DOCK ST
Old Dock
DEPARTURE
POINT
ARAN ISLAND
FERRY
New Pier
An Rinn Mhór
Rinmore Point
Mooring Posts
NIMMO'S PIER
1
2
3
42
GALWAY BAY
Cuan na Gaillimhe
A
B

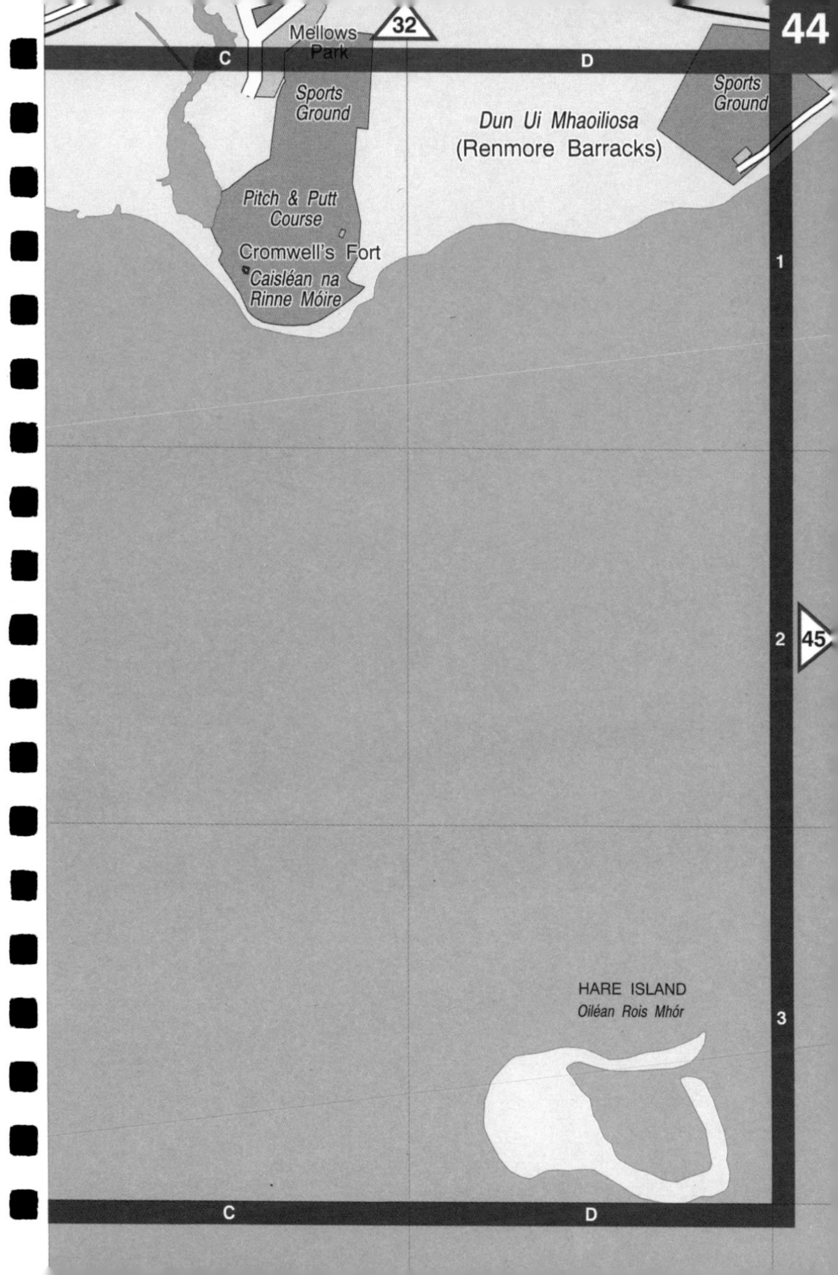
32
Mellows
Park
C
D
Sports
Ground
Dun Ui Mhaoiliosa
(Renmore Barracks)
Sports
Ground
Pitch & Putt
Course
Cromwell's Fort
Caisléan na
Rinne Móire
1
2
45
HARE ISLAND
Oiléan Rois Mhór
3
C
D

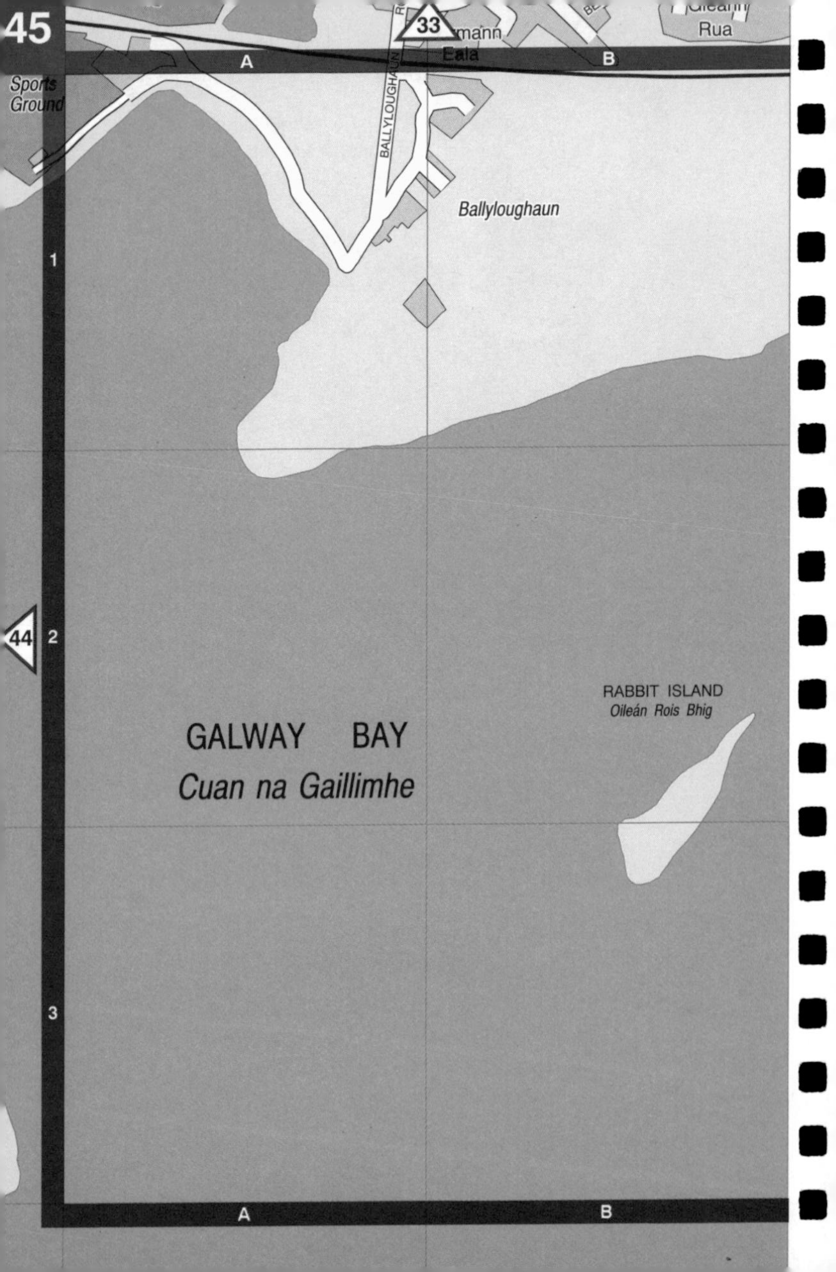

33
Eala
Rua
A
B
Sports Ground
BALLYLOUGHAUN
Ballyloughaun
1
44
2
3
RABBIT ISLAND
Oileán Rois Bhig
GALWAY BAY
Cuan na Gaillimhe
A
B

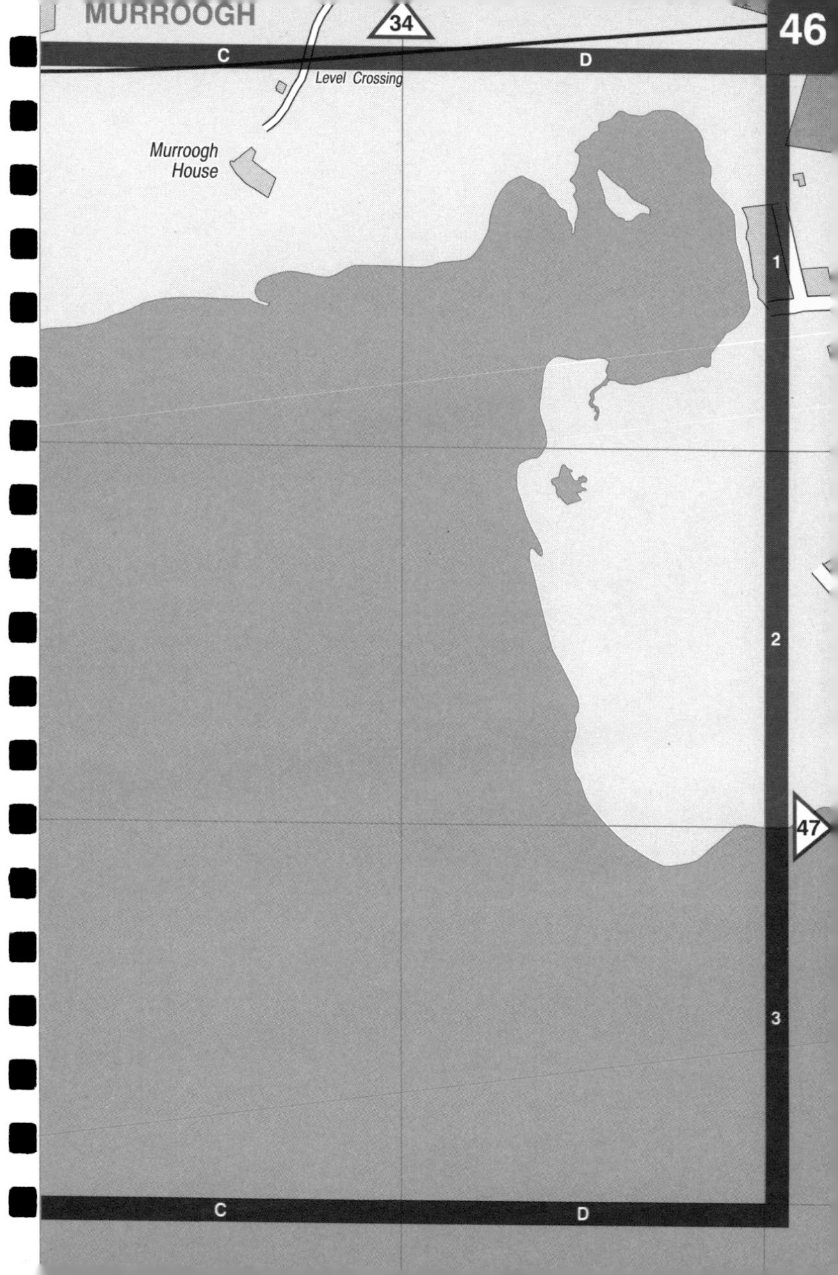
MURROOGH
34
C
D
Level Crossing
Murroogh House
1
2
47
3
C
D

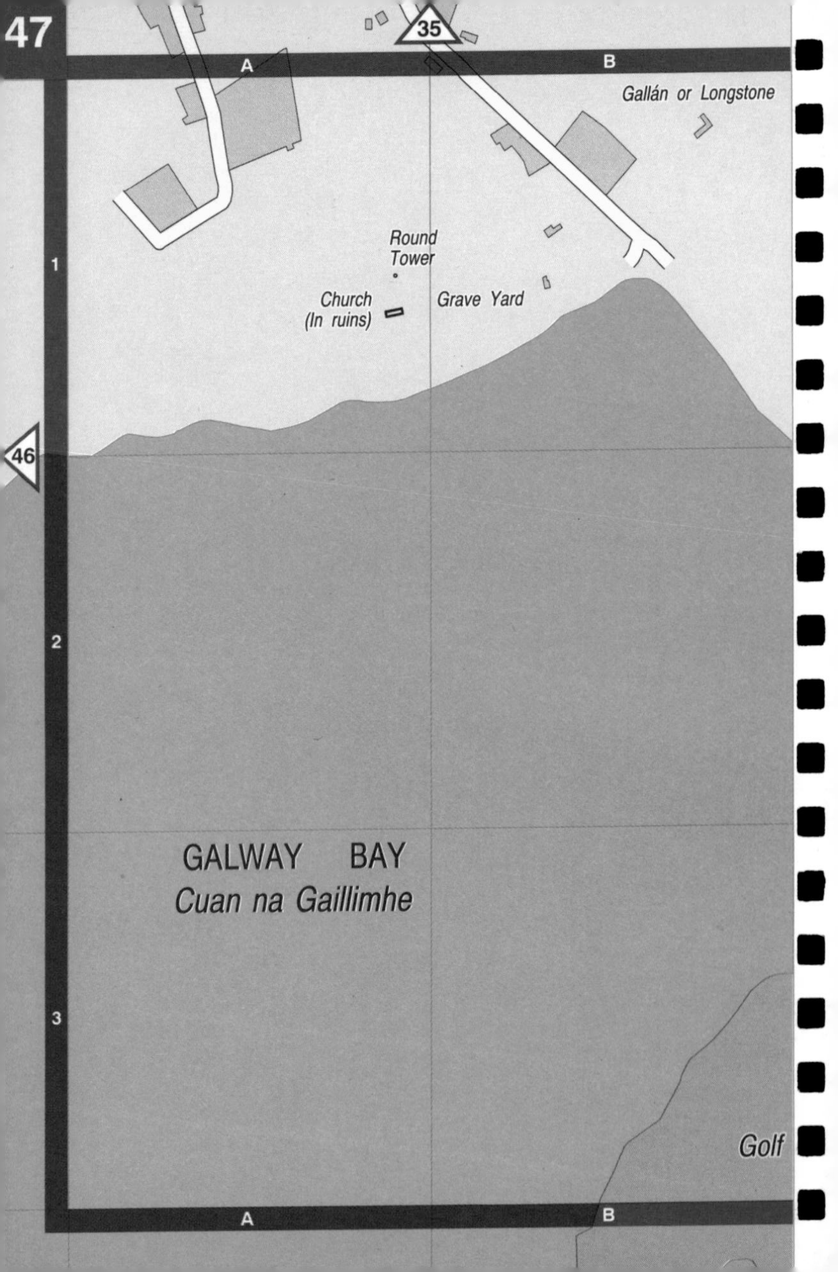
35
A
B
Gallán or Longstone
Round Tower
Church (In ruins)
Grave Yard
1
46
2
GALWAY BAY
Cuan na Gaillimhe
3
Golf
A
B

C D

ORANMORE BAY
Cuan Órán Mór

BLACK ISLANDS
Na hOileáin Dhubhan

1

Roscam Point
Ros Cam

2

3

BUNNABOLEY
Bun na Buaile

SALEEN
An Saílín

Course

C D

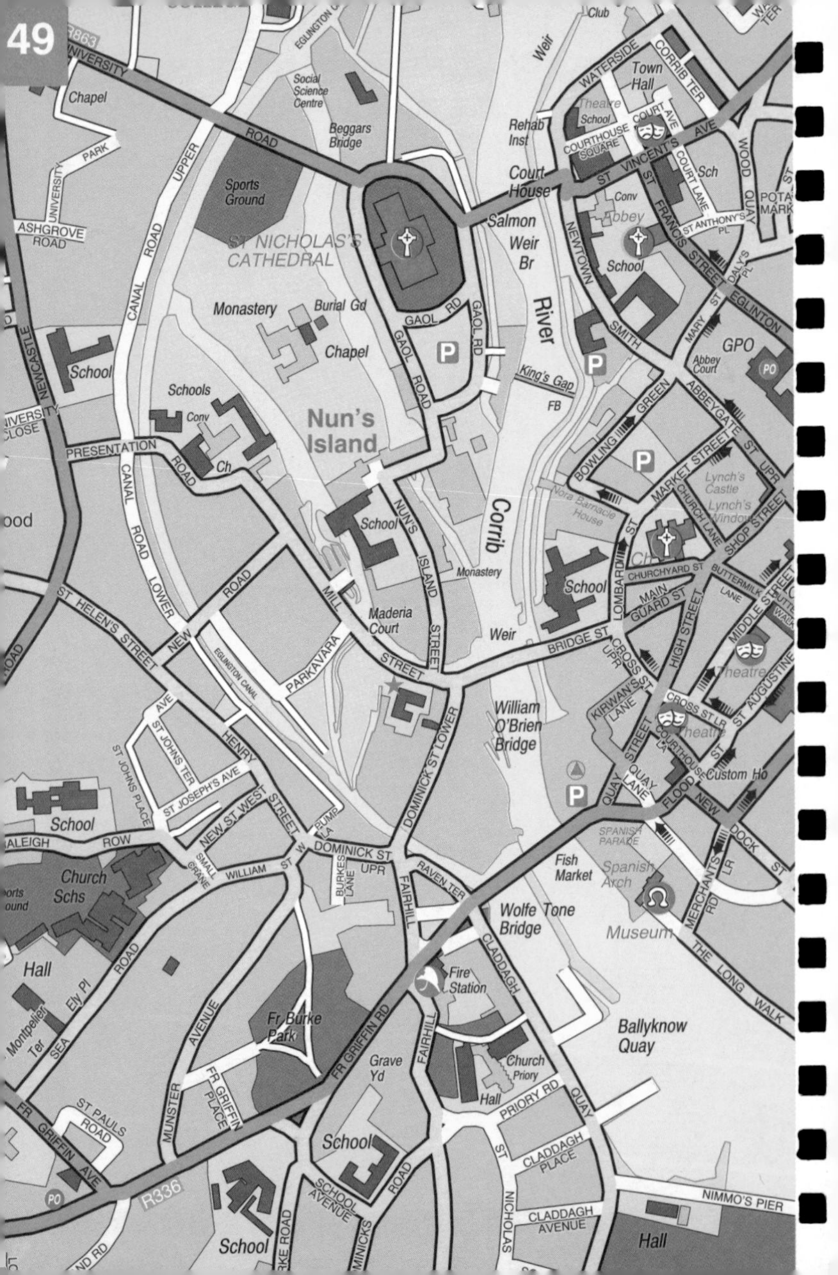
R863
UNIVERSITY ROAD
Chapel
UNIVERSITY PARK
ASHGROVE ROAD
EGLINTON CANAL
Social Science Centre
Beggars Bridge
Sports Ground
UPPER CANAL ROAD
ST NICHOLAS'S CATHEDRAL
Monastery
Burial Gd
Chapel
GAOL RD
GAOL ROAD
NEWCASTLE
School
Schools
Conv
UNIVERSITY CLOSE
PRESENTATION ROAD
Ch
Nun's Island
School
NUN'S ISLAND STREET
CANAL ROAD LOWER
MILL ROAD
Maderia Court
Monastery
Club
Weir
Rehab Inst
Court House
Salmon Weir Br
River
Corrib
King's Gap
FB
Weir
WATERSIDE
CORRIB TER
Town Hall
Theatre School
COURTHOUSE SQUARE
COURT AVE
ST VINCENT'S AVE
COURT LANE
Sch
WOOD QUAY
Conv
Abbey
NEWTOWN SMITH
ST FRANCIS STREET
ST ANTHONY'S PL
School
DALY'S PL
EGLINTON
MARY ST
GPO
PO
Abbey Court
ABBEYGATE ST UPR
BOWLING GREEN
MARKET STREET
Lynch's Castle
Lynch's Window
CHURCH LANE
SHOP STREET
Nora Barnacle House
School
LOMBARD ST
CHURCHYARD ST
BUTTERMILK LANE
MAIN GUARD ST
HIGH STREET
MIDDLE STREET
BRIDGE ST
CROSS ST UPR
Theatre
ST AUGUSTINE
ST HELEN'S STREET
NEW ROAD
EGLINTON CANAL
PARKAVARA
STREET
William O'Brien Bridge
KIRWAN'S LANE
CROSS ST LR
Theatre
COURTHOUSE LA
QUAY STREET
QUAY LANE
FLOOD ST
Custom Ho
NEW DOCK ST
AVE
ST JOHNS TER
ST JOHNS PLACE
HENRY STREET
ST JOSEPH'S AVE
NEW ST WEST
School
RALEIGH ROW
SMALL CRANE
WILLIAM ST W
RUMP LA
DOMINICK ST LOWER
DOMINICK ST UPR
BURKES LANE
FAIRHILL
RAVEN TER
SPANISH PARADE
Fish Market
Spanish Arch
MERCHANTS RD LR
Museum
THE LONG WALK
Church Schs
Sports Ground
Hall
Ely Pl
Montpelier Ter
SEA ROAD
AVENUE
Fr Burke Park
FR GRIFFIN RD
Wolfe Tone Bridge
CLADDAGH
Fire Station
FAIRHILL
Ballyknow Quay
Grave Yd
Church Priory
Hall
PRIORY RD
QUAY
FR GRIFFIN PLACE
MUNSTER
ST PAULS ROAD
FR GRIFFIN AVE
PO
R336
School
SCHOOL AVENUE
ROAD
CLADDAGH PLACE
ST NICHOLAS
NIMMO'S PIER
CLADDAGH AVENUE
Hall
School
DOMINICKS

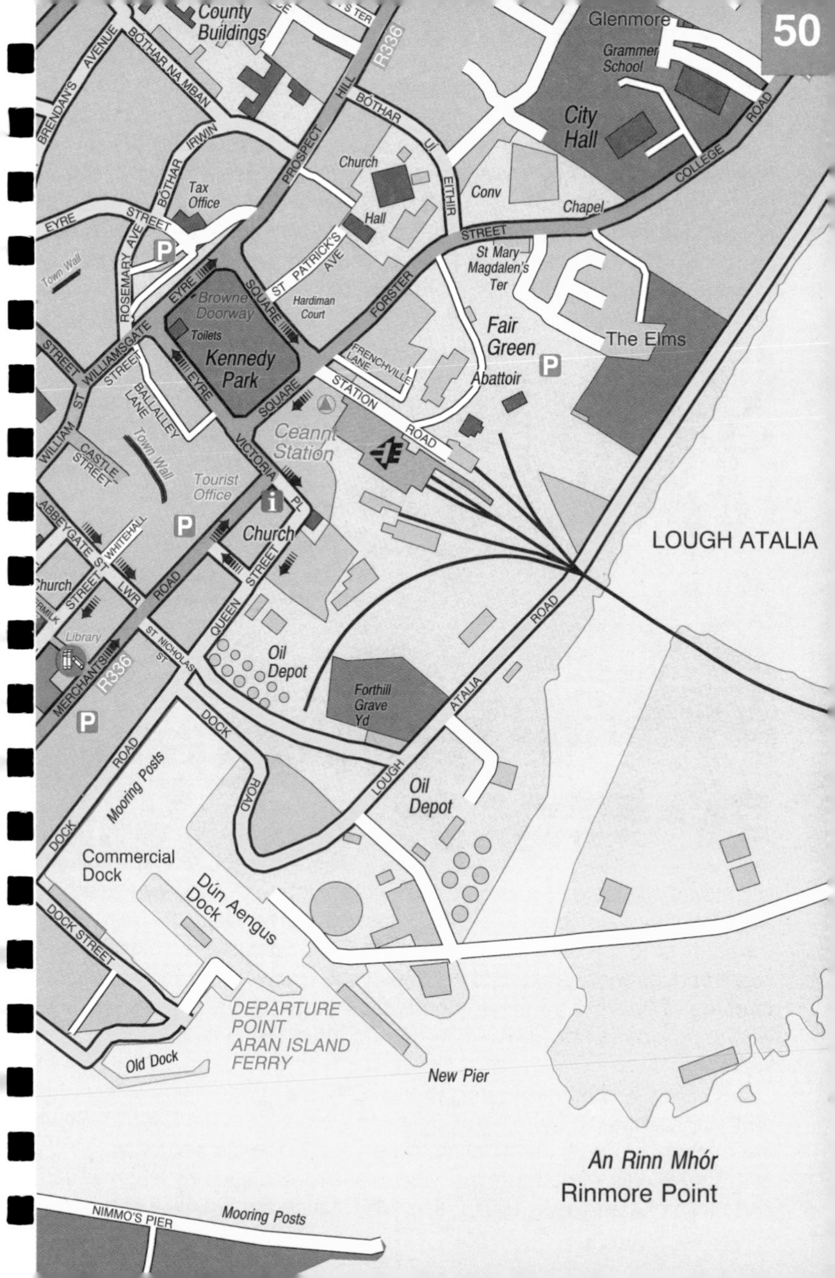
County Buildings
Glenmore
Grammer School
City Hall
BÓTHAR NA MBAN
BRENDAN'S AVENUE
R336
PROSPECT HILL
BÓTHAR UÍ EITHIR
COLLEGE ROAD
Church
Conv
Chapel
Tax Office
BÓTHAR IRWIN
EYRE STREET
Hall
ST PATRICK'S AVE
FORSTER STREET
St Mary Magdalen's Ter
Town Wall
ROSEMARY AVE
EYRE SQUARE
Browne Doorway
Toilets
Kennedy Park
Hardiman Court
Fair Green
The Elms
FRENCHVILLE LANE
STATION ROAD
Abattoir
WILLIAMSGATE STREET
BALLALLEY LANE
Ceannt Station
WILLIAM ST
CASTLE STREET
Town Wall
Tourist Office
VICTORIA PL
ABBEYGATE ST
WHITEHALL
Church
LOUGH ATALIA
Church
LWR ROAD
QUEEN STREET
Library
ST NICHOLAS ST
Oil Depot
MERCHANTS ROAD
Forthill Grave Yd
LOUGH ATALIA ROAD
DOCK ROAD
Mooring Posts
Oil Depot
Commercial Dock
Dún Aengus Dock
DOCK STREET
DEPARTURE POINT ARAN ISLAND FERRY
Old Dock
New Pier
An Rinn Mhór
Rinmore Point
NIMMO'S PIER
Mooring Posts

Galway - A Brief History

Galway takes its name from Galvia the mythological princess said to have drowned in the Galway River to which she also gave her name.

Although a town existed here from earliest times (probably the City of Magnata mentioned by Ptolemy). Galway is not a really old city. It was only during the period 1232-1243 that Galway became a town of any importance. When Richard de Burgo built a castle on the river between Lough Corrib and the sea a town soon grew up around it. Galway became a Royal borough in 1396 thus removing power from the de Burgos. The town was granted a royal charter in 1484 establishing its

city status. Despite its loyalty to the English crown Galway was ruled by wealthy "merchant princes". This was due to its isolation from other towns loyal to the crown and its largely Gaelic hinterland. These merchant princes were referred to in 1652 by the Cromwellian soldiers as the fourteen "Tribes". The most important of these was the Lynch family who supplied the first Mayor in 1484 and a further 83 over the next 169 years.

Galway was burned to the ground in 1473 and was rebuilt in the 16th and 17th Century. Many of the buildings were built in the Spanish Style the remains of which many can still be seen in the old city today.

Its fall was swift, however. Two disastrous sieges by Cromwellian and Williamite armies in 1651/2 and 1691 caused the demise of the city.

Its famous Tribes went into exile and, as trade the life blood of the ancient city, collapsed, the once proud city went into decline. A brief industrial recovery based on waterpower petered out in the 19th Century and it is only now that a real revival is evident.

Galway has long been an educational centre and in the 16th century it had the most renowned classical school in the country. Even now, the streets may be filled with students, for Galway is the city of the young with both its University and Institute of Technology supplying nearly a fifth of the population.

Relics of the city's former splendour can be seen in the many finely carved stone plaques, windows and doorways which stud the shop fronts; signs of Galway's bad times are now less obvious to be seen, due to Galway's renewal building in the last few years; evidence of the city's current revival can be seen in the activity in the very streets themselves

Claddagh

A visit to Galway is not complete, however, without a stroll through the old Claddagh fishing seafront on the western bank opposite the Spanish Arch. The small thatched homes are gone now, but the black hulls of fishing boats of Galway Hookers and Pucans, still contrast with the white swans of the Claddagh. While here, pay a visit to the Dominican Church and view its greatest treasure, the 17th Century wooden statue known as Our Lady of Galway. The world famous Claddagh ring owes its origins to this area of Galway.

Salthill

Once a small seaside resort 3km West of Galway, Salthill is now an important suburb of this expanding city. Salthill seems to have grown in importance as a result and today, it is the premier resort in Ireland. While it may have lost some of its simple, rural charms, it has gained a wealth of amenities in the process. The giant Leisureland complex, with its host of children's entertainment's, including an indoor heated swimming pool, proves very popular especially when the weather acts the spoilsport, as it will do at times here in the west. The golden half-mile of casinos, pubs and restaurants also play their part by day and discos and musical pubs rule the roost at night.

53

AN AERIAL VIEW OF GALWAY CITY

Browne Doorway
Eyre Square

This is a fine cut-stone doorway removed from its original position in 1905, from one of the old mansions in Lower Abbeygate Street. There are many carvings on the doorway including the coats of arms of the Browne Family.

Padraic O'Conaire Monument
Eyre Square

This monument sculptured by Albert Power R.H.A. was erected in 1935 to the memory of Padraic O'Conaire Gaelic writer and seanchaì.

Lynch's Castle
Shop Street

Situated on a corner where the two principal streets of ancient Galway City intersected. This is the finest surviving town castle in Ireland. The Castle is believed to have been built in the late 15th or early 16th century. There are many fine stonework features on the exterior of the castle including many coats of arms. Among the arms shown are those of the Lynchs, Fitzgeralds and King Henry VIII of England in whose reign the castle was built. The interior also contains many fine fireplaces. The castle now houses a bank.

Lynch Memorial Window
Market Street.

This gothic doorway is built into a re-erected house facade. On a black marble stone above the doorway an inscription reads "This memorial of the stern and unbending justice of the Chief Magistrate of this city James Lynch FitzStephens elected Mayor 1493 who condemned and executed his own guilty son Walter on this spot" FitzStephens

hanged his own son for murdering a visiting Spaniard out of jealously.

Nora Barnacle House
Bowling Green (Off Market Street)

Nora Barnacle who married James Joyce the internationally known author was born here in

1884. A memorial plaque was unveiled on the building in 1982 the 100th anniversary of James Joyce's birth. The Barnacle house is now a privately owned museum.

Collegiate Church of St. Nicholas.

Dedicated to St. Nicholas of Mgra was built by the Anglo-Norman's in 1320. The church which was made collegiate in 1484 was extended in 1486 and extended many times throughout the 16th century. There are many medieval relics and carvings contained in the Church. Christopher Columbus is said to have prayed here before his journey of discovery to the New World.

Blakes Castle

Situated at the end of Quay Street. The Castle is more correctly a tower house dating from the late 15th or early 16th century. It stands in or on the medieval city walls facing the old fishing village of the Claddagh on the opposite

side of the river. The castle having fallen into disrepair has been restored and now forms part of Jurys Hotel.

Spanish Arch

The arch does not form part of the old city wall. It was built as an extension to the wall as a protection for the quays below. These quays are where the Spanish

ships unloaded their cargoes of wine and brandy and is the most likely origin of its name. It is shown on Ordnance Survey maps as "The Blind Arch" the translation of An Poirse Caoch the name by which it is known to Irish Speakers.

Cathedral of Our Lady Assumed into Heaven and St. Nicholas

Designed by John L. Robinson and built between 1957 and 1965 on the site of the old county jail. Situated beside the Salmon Weir the Cathedral is of cut limestone from local quarries. In the interior the floors are of Connemara Marble. Above the altar in the

Chapel of St. Nicholas are three early 17th century carvings depicting the Coronation of the Virgin. The carvings were originally situated in the Collegiate Church of St. Nicholas

University College Galway.

Designed by Joseph B. Keane the foundation stone of this Tudor-style building was laid in 1846. The University was instituted in a Bill introduced to Parliament in 1845 by Sir Robert Peel and opened its doors to 68 students in 1849. It became a constituent college of the National University of Ireland in 1908.

The Library contains many rare books. Included among them are the Galway municipal records 1485-1818 and some purchased from Kings Inn Library in 1973 by An Taisce.

STREET INDEX

Street Name	Page/Grid Ref.
Abbey Court	30 D2[7]
Abbeygate St. Lower	31 A2
Abbeygate St. Upperr	30 D2
Aghnacurra	17 A1
Aille	25 A2
An Barnach	22 D1
An Cimín Mór	38 C1
An Culan	33 B1
An Lána Riabhach	37 B3
Arbutus Avenue	32 D2
Ard Aoibhinn Drive	21 B3
Ard Fraoigh	27 A2
Ardilaun Road	17 B3
Ardmore	28 D3
Ardmore Road	29 A2
Árd Na Coille	29 A3
Árd Na Mara	41 A1
Ash Road	29 B1
Ashbrook	20 D2
Ashdale Road	29 A3
Ashfield Road	17 B2
Ashgrove	38 D1
Ashgrove Road	30 C2
Ashleigh Grove	38 D1
Avondale Road	29 A2
Atlantic Terrace	41 A2
Averard West	29 B3
Ballagh	4 C3
Ballagh Road	3 B3
Ballalley Lane	31 A2
Ballard	37 A1
Ballinfoile Mews	20 C1
Ballinfoile Park	7 B3
Ballintemple	12 D2
Ballybaan	21 B2
Ballybaan Road	21 B2
Ballybrit	22 C1
Ballybrit Court	22 D2
Ballybrit Heights	22 D1
Ballybrit Race Course	10 D3
Ballyburke	26 D2
Ballyknow Quay	30 D3
Ballyloughaun	33 B3
Ballyloughaun Road	33 B2
Ballymoneen	26 C3
Ballymoneen Road	26 D2
Barna Road	37 A3
Barna Road	38 D2
Barry Avenue	21 A2
Barr Aille	20 D1
Barr Na Carraige	28 C3
Barr Na Cluana	19 B1
Bayview Heights	21 B3
Bayview Rise	21 B3
Beach Avenue	33 B2
Beach Avenue	41 A2
Beach Close	33 B2
Beach Court	42 C1
Beach Drive	33 B2
Beattystown	42 D1
Beechmount Avenue	29 A3
Beechmount Road	29 A2
Beechpark	33 A2
Beechwood Park	21 B3
Belmont	33 B1
Belsize Court	17 A3
Bishop O'Donnell Road	28 D3
Blackthorn Park	33 A2
Blake's Hill	39 A2
Blake's Lane	31 A1
Bohermore	31 A1
Boleybeg	13 B3
Boleybeg East	13 A2
Boleynasruhaun	2 C2
Bóthar Colmain	30 C2
Bóthar Einde	30 C2
Bóthar Irwin	31 A1
Bóthar Le Chéile	29 A1
Bóthar Na Dtreabh	19 B2
Bóthar Na Dtreabh	21 A1
Bóthar Na Dtreabh	23 B2
Bóthar Na mBan	31 A1
Bóthar Mhic Concairrge	29 B2
Bóthar Phádraic Uì Chonnaire	29 B2
Bóthar Uì Eithir	31 A1
Bóthar Uì Roideacháin	29 B2
Bowling Green	30 D2
Breanloughaun	12 C2
Briar Hill	23 A2
Bridge St	30 D2
Brockagh	11 B1
Brookdale	19 B1
Brooklawn	39 B1
Bruach Na Mara	39 A2
Bunnaboley	48 C3
Burkes Lane	30 D3
Burren View Heights	39 B2
Bushy Park	4 D3
Bushy Park Lawn	17 A1
Buttermilk Lane	30 D2[2]
Buttermilk Walk	30 D2[3]
Cabbage Lane	31 A1
Caiseal Mara	39 A2
Camillaun Park	29 A1
Canal Road Lower	30 C2
Canal Road Upper	30 C2
Cappagh	25 B1
Cappagh Road	25 B2
Cappanaveagh	41 A2
Carbry Road	29 B1
Cardinal Cushing Rd	33 A1
Carn Ard	28 D1
Carragh Close	39 A2
Carragh Court	39 B2
Carragh Drive	39 A2
Carragh Hill	39 B1
Carraig Ard	28 D3
Carraig Bán	7 A3
Carrigeen	27 A3
Cashel Court	39 B2
Castle Street	31 A2
Castlegar	9 A2
Castlelawn Heights	19 A2
Castlepark	22 C2
Castlepark Road	22 C2
Cedarwood Close	29 A2
Cherry Park	17 A2
Chestnut Close	33 A2
Chestnut Lane	4 D3
Churchfields	41 B1
Church Lane	30 D2[4]
Churchyard Street	30 D2[5]
Cill Ard	31 A1
Circular Road	16 D3
Circular Rd. Cottages	28 D1
Claddagh	42 D1
Claddagh Avenue	30 D3
Claddagh Place	30 D3
Claddagh Quay	30 D3
Claremont	28 D1
Clareview Park	22 C3
Clark Avenue	21 A2
Clifton Avenue	17 B2
Clifton Close	17 B1
Clifton Crescent	17 B2
Clifton Drive	17 B2
Clifton Park	17 B2
Cloghscoltia	16 C2
Cluain Airne	39 A1
Cluain Ard	22 C2
Cluain Dara	26 D3
Cluain Fada	20 C1
Cluain Mhór	27 A3
Clybaun	27 B2
Clybaun Heights	39 A1
Clybaun Road	27 A1
Clybaun Road	39 A1
Cnoc na Cille	22 C2
Cnoc an Óir	28 D1
Cois Cuain Apartments	41 B1
College Road	31 B1

Colmcille Road 29 B2
Connolly Avenue 21 A2
Cookes Terrace 19 B3
Coolagh 7 A2
Coolagh 23 B1
Coolagh Road 6 D3
Coole Park 19 B3
Corcullen 1 A1
Corrib Park 17 B3
Corrib Terrace 30 D1[1]
Corrib Village 18 C2
Costelloe Road 29 B2
Court Avenue 30 D1
Court Lane 30 D1
Courthouse Lane 30 D2[1]
Courthouse Square 30 D1
Crescent Green 30 C3
Crescent View 20 D1
Crestwood 19 A1
Cross Street Lower 30 D2
Cross Street Upper 30 D2
Cruachan Park 28 C2
Cuan na Coille 28 D3
Cuar Nalus 28 D1
Cúl Ard 20 D3
Curralee 19 B1
Dalton Drive 41 A1
Dalton Place 29 A3
Daly's Place 30 D2
Dalysfort Road 41 A1
Dangan 17 A2
Dangan Court 17 A1
Dangan Heights 17 A1
Davis Road 29 B2
Devon Court 29 A3
Devon Gardens 41 A1
Devon Mews 29 A3
Devon Park 41 A1
Devon Place 30 C3
Distillery Road 18 C3
Dock Road 31 A3
Dock Street 31 A3
Doctor Colohan Road 41 B1
Doctor Mannix Avenue 41 A1
Doctor Mannix Drive 41 A1
Doctor Mannix Road 40 D1
Doire Gheal 27 B3
Dominick Street Lower 30 D3
Dominick Street Upper 30 D3
Doughiska Road 23 B3
Doughiska Road 36 C2
Drom Óir 26 D3
Drum East 13 B1
Drum West 1 A3
Dún Daingean 17 A1
Dublin Road 20 C3
Dublin Road 33 A1
Dún a Rì 39 A1
Dún Na Mara 32 D2
Dún Na Mara Drive 32 D2
Dyke Road 18 D3
Eastern Approach Road 36 D1
Eglington Street 30 D2
Elm Park 33 A2
Elmpark Road 17 B2
Ely Place 30 C3
Emerson Avenue 41 A1
Emmet Avenue 21 A2
Eyre Square 31 A2
Eyre Street 31 A2
Fairhill 30 D3
Fair Green 31 A2
Fairlands Park 17 B2
Flood Street 30 D3
Forest Hills 38 D1
Forster Court 31 A1
Forster Street 31 A2
Fort Lorenzo 28 C3
Foster Park 41 A1
Fr Burke Road 42 D1
Fr Griffin Avenue 30 C3
Fr Griffin Place 30 C3
Fr Griffin Road 30 D3
Frenchville 42 D1
Frenchville Lane 31 A2
Friar's Hill 28 D2
Fursey Road 29 B2
Fuschia Drive 33 A2
Fuschia Park 33 A2
Gaol Road 30 D2
Geata Na Mara 34 C1
Gentian Hill 39 A3
Gleann Bhán 22 D2
Gleann Dara 28 D2
Gleann Na Coille 37 B2
Gleann Rua 33 B2
Glenanail Drive 20 C2
Glenard Avenue 40 D1
Glenard Crescent 40 D1
Glenard Road 40 D1
Glenavon Drive 22 C2
Glenburren Park 21 A1
Gaelcarraig Park 17 A3
Glenina Heights 33 A1
Glenmore 31 B1
Glenvale Court 27 A3
Glen View Drive 20 C1
Gortatleva 3 A2
Gortcam 22 C2
Gorteennafolla 16 D1
Gort Gréine 28 C2
Gort Rua 26 D3
Grangemore 28 C2
Grattan Court 30 C3
Grattan Park 42 C1
Grattan Road 41 B1
Grattan Road 42 C1
Grattan Terrace 42 D1
Grealishtown 19 B3
Greenfields 17 B2
Greenfields Road 17 B2
Greenview Heights 29 A1
Gurteen 32 D1
Gurthard Avenue 40 D2
Hardiman Court 31 A2[2]
Hawthorn Drive 32 D2
Hawthorn Place 27 A2
Hazel Park 17 A2
Haxelwood 28 D3
Headford Road 8 C1
Headford Road 19 B1
Headford Road 31 A1
Heather Grove 21 B3
Henry Street 30 C2
Highfield Park 29 A2
High Street 30 D2
Hillcrest Court 39 B2
Hillside Park 22 D3
Holly Grove 33 A2
Hy-Brasil Court 17 A3
Illaunacorra 6 D3
Inchagoill Road 17 B3
Inishannagh Park 29 A1
Jordan's Island 18 C2
James Connolly Tce. 31 B1
John Coogan Park 29 A1
Keeraun 26 C1
Kent Avenue 21 A2
Kentfield 3 B2
Killeen 3 B1
Kings Hill 41 A2
Kingston 39 B1
Kingston Gardens 39 B1
Kirwan's Lane 30 D2
Knockadoney 16 C1
Knockaunnacarrach 37 A3
Knockayarragh 7 B2
Knock Na Brona 16 C2
Knocknacarra 39 B2
Knocknacarra Park 39 A1
Knocknacarra Road 39 B2
Knocknafraska 16 C1
Kylemore Park 29 B3
Laghtavarna 9 A3
Lake Shore Drive 32 C2

Lake View Road 17 B2
Lakewood Park 18 D2
Larchfield Avenue 33 A2
Laurel Park 17 A3
Leitriff Road 14 C1
Leitriff Road 16 C3
Lenaboy 41 A1
Lenaboy Avenue 41 A2
Lenaboy Gardens 41 A1
Lenaboy Park 41 B1
Letteragh 16 D3
Liam Mellows Terrace 19 B3
Lisbeg Lawn 33 A2
Lisheenakeeran 1 A2
Lios Caisil 22 D1
Lioscarraig 40 C2
Lios Ealtan 30 C3
Liosmore 37 B1
Lombard Street 30 D2
Lough Atalia Avenue 32 D2
Lough Atalia Grove 32 D1
Lough Atalia Road 31 B1
Loughnane Place 21 A3
Loughnane Terrace 21 A3
Loyola Park 20 C3
Loyola Place 30 C3
Lurgan Park 34 C2
Lus Leana 20 C1
Lydon Terrace 19 B3
Maderia Court 30 D2
Main Guard Street 30 D2
Mallin Avenue 21 A3
Manor Avenue 28 C3
Manor Close 28 C3
Manor Court 26 C3
Manor Drive 28 C3
Market Street 30 D2
Mary's Street 30 D2
Maunsells Park 29 B2
Maunsells Road 29 B2
McBride Avenue 21 B2
McDara Road 29 B2
McDermott Avenue 21 A2
McDonagh Avenue 21 A2
McDonagh Terrace 30 D1[2]
McHugh Avenue 21 B3
Meadow Grove 21 B2
Mellows Park 32 C2
Menlough 5 B1
Merchants Road 31 A2
Merchants Road Lr. 30 D3
Michael Collins Road 21 A3
Middle Street 30 D2
Mill Street 30 D2
Millers Lane 28 C3
Monalee Heights 38 D1
Monalee Manor 38 C1
Moneenageisha Cross 20 C3
Moneenageisha Road 20 C3
Monivea Park 21 B2
Monivea Road 21 A2
Monksfield 41 A2
Montpelier Terrace 30 C3
Monument Road 6 C1
Mount Pleasant Drive 29 A2
Moyola Park 17 B3
Munster Avenue 30 C3
Murroogh 34 C2
Murrough Avenue 33 B2
Murrough Drive 33 B2
Murrough Park 33 B2
Na Cúillíní 40 D1
New Avenue 29 A2
New Dock Street 30 D3
New Road 30 C2
New Street West 30 C3
Newcastle 17 B3
Newcastle Avenue 30 C1
Newcastle Park 30 C1
Newcastle Road 30 C2
Newcastle Road Lower 30 C1
Newtown Smith 30 D2
Nimmo's Pier 30 D3
Nun's Island 30 D2
Nun's Island Street 30 D2
Oaklands 41 A1
Oakley Crescent 29 A2
Oakwood Close 30 C2
Ocean Tower Apartments 40 C2
Ocean Wave 41 B1
O'Flaherty Road 29 B2
Old Dublin Road 35 B2
Oldfield 39 B1
Oranhill 3 A1
Palmyra Avenue 30 C3
Palmyra Park 30 C3
Parkavarra 30 D2
Park Avenue 41 A2
Parkmore 9 B3
Parkmore Industrial Est. 11 A1
Parknagapple 3 B3
Parnell Avenue 21 A2
Pearse Avenue 21 A2
Pinewood Grove 33 A2
Plunkett Avenue 21 A2
Pollacushlaun 36 D3
Pollboy 36 D1
Pollinapreaghaun 8 D2
Pollnarooma 40 C1
Pollnarooma West 39 B1
Port a Carron 26 D3
Potato Market 30 D1
Presentation Road 30 C2
Priory Road 30 D3
Prospect Hill 31 A1
Pump Lane 30 D3
Quay Lane 30 D3
Quay Street 30 D3
Quincentennial Drive 41 A2
Queen Street 31 A2
Quinn Place 21 A3
Quinn Terrace 21 A3
Racecourse Gardens 22 D1
Racecourse Lawn 22 D1
Rahylin Glebe 21 B3
Rahoon 28 D2
Rahoon Park North 28 D2
Rahoon Park South 28 D2
Rahoon Road 13 B3
Rahoon Road 27 B1
Rahoon Road 29 A2
Raleigh Road 30 C3
Raven Terrace 30 D3
Renmore 33 A2
Renmore Avenue 33 A1
Renmore Crescent 32 C2
Renmore Park 32 D1
Renmore Road 32 D2
Revagh Road 40 D2
Rivendell 29 A3
Riverside Estate 20 D1
Riverside View 20 C2
Rockbarton Green 40 D1
Rockbarton North 40 D2
Rockbarton Park 40 D2
Rockbarton Road 40 D1
Rockbarton West 40 D2
Rock Field Park 28 D2
Rockhill Avenue 41 A1
Rockland's Avenue 21 B2
Rockmount Road 29 A2
Ros Árd 38 C1
Rosary Lane 29 A3
Roscam 35 B3
Roscam Park 36 C2
Rosedale 28 D3
Roselyn Gardens 33 A2
Rosemary Avenue 31 A2
Ros Geal 28 C2
Rosmeen Court 41 B1
Rosnashee 19 A2
Rowan Avenue 33 A2
Rusheen Woods 39 A1
Rutledge Terrace 40 D2
Saleen 48 D3

Street	Page / Grid
Salthill	41 B1
Salthill Road Lower	41 B1
Salthill Road Upper	40 D2
Salthill Road Upper	41 A2
San Antonio Terrace	41 A2
Sandy Road	19 B2
Sandyvale Lawn	19 B2
Sandy View Drive	20 C2
School Avenue	30 D3
Seacrest	38 D1
Seacrest	38 D2
Seagrove	33 B2
Seaman Drive	20 C1
Seamount	40 C2
Seamus Quirke Road	29 A2
Sean Mulvoy Road	19 A3
Seapoint Promenade	41 B2
Sea Road	30 C3
Shangort Park	39 A1
Shangort Road	38 D1
Shantalla Place	29 B2
Shantalla Road	29 B2
Shantallow	29 B2
Sherwood Avenue	30 C3
Shop Street	30 D2
Siobhán McKenna Road	17 A3
Sliabh Rua	22 D3
SlíNa Sruthán	27 A2
Small Crane	30 C3[2]
Snipe Avenue	18 C3
Snipe Lawn	18 C3
South Park Place	30 D3
South Park Terrace	42 D1
Spanish Parade	30 D3
Spire Gardens	29 B2
Station Road	31 A2
St Anthony's Place	30 D2[6]
St Anthony's Terrace	19 B3
St Augustine Street	30 D2
St Brendan's Avenue	31 A1
St Bridget's Court Lr.	31 A1[2]
St Bridget's Place	31 A1
St Bridget's Place Lr.	31 A1[1]
St Bridget's Place Upr.	31 A1
St Bridget's Terrace	31 A1
St Dominick's Avenue	42 D1
St Dominick's Road	30 D3
St Finbarr's Terrace	19 A3
St Francis Street	30 D1
St Helen's Street	30 C2
St Ignatius Terrace	42 D1
St James Crescent	21 A3
St James Road	21 B3
St John's Avenue	30 C2[1]
St John's Place	30 C3[1]
St John's Terrace	30 C2
St Joseph's Avenue	30 C3
St Joseph's Terrace	29 B3
St Mary Magdalen's Tce.	31 B2
St Mary's Avenue	29 B3
St Mary's Park	29 B3
St Mary's Terrace	29 B3
St Mary's Road	30 C3
St Nicholas Road	30 D3
St Nicholas Street	31 A2[1]
St Vincent's Avenue	30 D1
St Patrick's Avenue	31 A2
St Paul's Road	30 C3
St Ronan's Close	40 D2
Suncroft Court	29 B3
Sycamore Court	32 D2
Sycamore Drive	29 A3
Sylvan Avenue	17 B2
Sylvan Close	17 B2
Sylvan Drive	17 B2
Sylvan Grove	17 B2
Sylvan Heights	17 B2
Sylvan Road	17 B2
Tara Grove	20 D3
Taylor's Hill Road	28 D3
Taylor's Hill Road	29 B3
Tearmann Eala	33 B2
Terryland	19 A2
The Bailey	17 A2
The Crescent	30 C3
The Elms	31 B2
The Gardens	28 C3
The Green	31 B1
The Heath	16 D2
The Links	38 C1
The Long Walk	30 D3
The Maples	41 A1
The Meadows	22 D1
The Nurseries	29 B3
The Orchard	28 C3
The Rise	26 D3
The Village	20 C3
Thomas Hynes Road	17 B3
Threadneedle Road	40 D1
Tirellan Heights	19 A1
Tonabrocky	14 C2
Tonacurragh	4 C1
Tone Avenue	21 A2
Townparks	19 A3
Tuam Road	10 C1
Tuam Road	20 C3
Tuam Road	21 A1
Tudor Close	38 D1
Tudor Lawn	17 A2
Tulach Ard	28 D1
Twomileditch	10 D1
University Close	30 C2
University Park	30 C1
University Road	30 C1
Upper Newcastle	18 C3
Upper Salthill	40 C2
Victoria Place	31 A2
Walsh's Terrace	30 D1
Walter Macken Place	21 A3
Walter Macken Road	21 A3
Water Lane	31 A1
Waterside	30 D1
Wellpark	20 D3
Wellpark Grove	20 D3
Wellpark Road	20 C3
Westbrook	38 C1
Whitehall	31 A2
Whitestrand Avenue	29 B3
Whitestrand Park	42 C1
Whitestrand Road	42 C1
Whitethorn Close	32 D2
William Street	31 A2
William Street West	30 C3
Williamsgate Street	31 A2
Willow Park	30 C2
Windfield Gardens	27 A3
Woodfield	38 C2
Woodhaven	34 C1
Woodland's Avenue	32 D1
Woodland's Green	32 D1
Wood Quay	30 D1
Woodmount	41 A2
Woodview Court	38 D1
Yewland Green	33 A2

LIST OF STREETS NOT NAMED ON MAP AND SHOWN BY SMALL NUMBERS

Page / Gr. Ref		Street Name
30 C2	1	St John's Avenue
30 C3	1	St John's Place
	2	Small Crane
30 D1	1	Corrib Terrace
	2	Mcdonagh Terrace
30 D2	1	Courthouse Lane
	2	Buttermilk Lane
	3	Buttermilk Walk
	4	Church Lane
	5	Churchyard Street
	6	St Anthony's Place
	7	Abbey Court
31 A1	1	St Bridget's Place Lr
	2	St Bridget's Court Lr
31 A2	1	St Nicholas Street
	2	Hardiman Court